FINDING
THE
MISSING
PIECES

*How to Solve the
Puzzle of Digital
Modernization and
Transformation*

Jim Lambert

Contents

Preface

Hope springs eternal. Every time a Transformation begins there is always a feeling of hope and excitement for what the future will bring. But as the Universe is wont to do, our best laid plans are always met with unexpected and challenging twists and turns. In the midst of ever-changing circumstances, we are continually presented with new obstacles to overcome and new problems to solve. The journey seems to be unfolding per its own will, not ours, and reality repeatedly shows us that it refuses to be controlled or denied. By not embracing the fact that everything around us is constantly changing and temporary, we end up creating difficulties for ourselves by desperately and blindly clinging to our original thoughts and plans. Regardless of how often reality blocks our path and tries to guide us in a different direction, we do not seem to be getting the message. The world is demanding that we surrender to 'what is' and adapt accordingly, yet we continue to fight against it. This is a losing battle. As Carl Jung once said, *'what you resist not only persists, it will grow in size'*. This problem has definitely grown in size. It is time to stop resisting.

Over the last several decades I have worked with many companies that launched major initiatives for Modernization and Transformation. Many of them struggled to see the realities that emerged before them along the way. Some seemed to enter into a state of denial when those initiatives sputtered and failed, oftentimes claiming some sort of superficial victory when no true business value had been realized. It was this continuing pattern of coming up short, seen across companies of all shapes and sizes, that led me to question exactly why we are collectively stuck in a seemingly infinite loop where we do not learn from our failures and make appropriate adjustments. While failure can be enormously frustrating, it is consistently one of the best teachers in life. But repeatedly failing while using the same approaches and thinking is, in the words of Albert Einstein, the definition of insanity. Organizations continue to undertake the most well-intentioned Modernization and Transformation initiatives but are continually thwarted. We need to expand our thinking before we can move forward.

Through working with a myriad of different companies and leadership teams, I would say that many of their struggles to successfully transform could be described by the idea that 'you don't know what you don't know'. Collectively companies, consultants, and business academics are all doing their best, but they consistently are looking within their own organizations, or to each other, for what they believe to be the best ways to achieve their transformational objectives. Looking exclusively within the business world 'bubble' for answers is inherently limited. There are generally consistent and well-known approaches that reflect a shared level of knowledge and self-awareness. Remaining in this 'bubble' has resulted in the recycling and restating of what are basically the same ideas and methods, most of which are focused on certain *parts* of what ultimately contributes to successful transformations. These types of viewpoints typically do not consider the broader forces at play in business and in life, especially the impacts of the individual biases, beliefs, and behaviors that exist in everyone from company leaders to front-line employees. There is an opportunity to leverage what we already know and build on top of it, creating an expanded approach that treats these factors as being equally integral to success. Providing a way for companies to learn more about 'what you don't know', we can come upon a newly revealed path on our journey that leads to further growth and maturity, and thereby transformational success.

The goal of this book is to present a different way of thinking about and approaching Modernization and Transformation efforts that is intended to increase the chances and rate of success. It is disheartening to watch people, teams and companies continue to struggle, fail, and become disillusioned while squandering so much time, effort, and funding along the way. Collectively we could benefit from staging some sort of intervention that will break the cycle. This book provides a new perspective from which to approach these complex initiatives. My sincere hope is that the reader finds value in applying some or all of this framework in their own context and that it aids their efforts to achieve success. As an Agilist at heart, and in the spirit of the Agile Manifesto - here's to uncovering better ways of working by doing it and helping others do it, as we truly need each other's help to be more successful going forward than we are today.

- Jim Lambert
Denver, Colorado, 20 May 2021
First Edition

Acknowledgements

There are many academics, scholars and philosophers that have greatly influenced the content of this book. The main inspiration behind the framework presented herein can be attributed to Ken Wilber's collective works regarding Integral Theory. Integral Theory incorporates and synthesizes the extensive work of a wide variety of human development theories. The list below are specific individuals and their concepts that are reflected in Wilber's books as well as within these pages:

- Dr. Clare W. Graves - *Emergent Cyclical Theory and Values*
- Don Edward Beck and Christopher C. Cowan - *Spiral Dynamics*
- Jean Piaget - *Cognitive Capacities*
- Richard Dawkins - *Memetics*
- Jean Gebser - *Structures of Consciousness and Worldviews*
- Frederic Laloux - *Reinventing Organizations*
- Abraham Maslow - *Hierarchy of Needs*
- Jane Loevinger - *Self-Identity and Stages of Ego Development*
- C. G. Jung - *Individuation and Shadow*
- Erik Erikson - *Stages of Psychosocial Development*
- Lawrence Kohlberg - *Stages of Moral Development*

Anyone familiar with the collective works of this group will clearly see that they are direct inspirations and sources of the quadrant-stages-developmental lines framework presented in this book. It is with the greatest gratitude that I give credit to where credit is truly due, as I am writing this on the backs of giants.

In their own ways, each of these thinkers and their resulting models incorporated concepts of individual maturity alongside a comprehensive history and analysis of overall human evolution and development. In this well-established scientific thinking of human progress, our evolution as a species is viewed as being comprised of personal, physical, cultural, and social structures and stages. The key being that both individuals and humanity as a whole periodically makes a 'leap' by fully integrating prior stages while also transcending them to reach the next stage. The same holds true when applied to the topics of business and technology, as they both reflect our own collective human development and progress. By looking outside of the 'business bubble' we can learn much from these thought models which can be brought in and effectively applied to our efforts and increase the chances for transformational success.

Finding the Missing Pieces

How to Solve the Puzzle of Digital Modernization and Transformation

A Culture of Failure

Adapt or Die.

Humankind has been driven by this maxim throughout its existence. Those three words represent a truth that has been our reality long before it was ever written down as a specific scientific theory. In his 1859 publication, *On the Origin of Species*, Charles Darwin presented the idea that those species that adapt best to their changing environment have the best chance of surviving, while those who do not adapt simply do not continue to exist. This Theory of Natural Selection was famously restated by Leon C. Megginson, a Professor of Management and Marketing, as:

> *"It is not the strongest of the species that survives, nor the most intelligent that survives. It is the one most adaptable to change."[1]*

This basic concept has become a hallmark of the business world today. With notions of evolution and survival being incorporated into company strategies around the world, the terms **Modernization** and **Transformation** have in turn become virtually inescapable throughout every boardroom, planning session, and market or industry analysis out there. Fearing for their organization's continued existence, company executives feel compelled to take action before it is too late.

Those actions become bold attempts to adapt to the increasingly volatile, complex, and rapidly changing world in which they operate. Large scale initiatives with significant organizational, cultural, and technological impacts are happening across all industries and sectors. Many of the programs carry with them the hopes of bringing their companies further into a new modern age in which they can reap untold rewards, while for many others it is the means by which to simply ensure their continued success and survival.

This drive for survival is not without its dangers and pitfalls. Similar to Evolution and Natural Selection, Modernization and Transformation are relatively simple and generic terms that in fact represent a staggering level of underlying complexity. As Modernization and Transformation programs have become more and more commonplace, it has also become somewhat of a standard practice to add other words to their names like 'Organizational', 'DevOps', 'Agile', 'Cultural', or the most well-known, 'Digital'. Early on describing an initiative as 'Digital Modernization' or 'Digital Transformation' might have been a way to provide more specificity to what these programs entail, but the truth is that regardless of the label used, it still belies a scope of work that goes far beyond the 'digital' technology considerations. Digital Modernization and Digital Transformation programs both have a strong focus on using technology to improve business results, but it is important to understand that in companies where these initiatives have indeed been successful, the programs themselves have been much broader undertakings. They have gone beyond 'Digital' to address the entire organization and its unique needs. With the variety of companies that exist of all sizes across all industries and geographies, the specific types and scope of these initiatives can be enormously diverse and wide ranging. Which is precisely why most people continue to struggle with defining exactly what is meant by a term such as 'Digital Transformation'.

To be clear, there are certain differences in the commonly understood and implied definitions of Modernization and Transformation. Modernization typically equates to replacing outdated legacy systems while Transformation often encompasses changes to business structures and practices internally as well as externally with customers and partners. *Digital Modernization* is normally thought of as being focused on the adoption of new technology, involving the upgrading of systems, platforms, and software to meet today's modern needs. It can be as simple as taking an existing paper process and making it electronic by using new software and hardware, or more complex, such as phasing out existing infrastructure and equipment and moving to the cloud. *Digital Transformation* frequently means taking advantage of new and innovative technologies in ways that might lead companies to reimagine organizational processes, culture, people, and customer experiences. These efforts can directly result in more significant organizational adaptations such as entirely new business models, revenue streams, policies, and values. While *Digital Modernization* might be focused on bringing an organization "up to speed" with the latest technology, *Digital Transformation* may require looking at the organization through a holistic lens and shaking up the business model to fundamentally change business performance. No matter what the specific terms or scope are in each individual case, these are all forms of evolutionary progress in the name of continued survival. For many of these companies the drive is to not merely survive, but to thrive. This is why the Modernization and Transformation topics have taken on increased meaning and importance with such a large number of company leaders, stakeholders, and strategists.

Seeing the amount of activity, research, and reporting in this space it is abundantly clear that most senior executives recognize the need for their companies to be able to adapt effectively. To that end they are including Modernization and Transformation initiatives in their overall strategies. A vast majority of CEOs recently surveyed by Gartner said they have a Modernization or Transformation effort currently underway[2]. There are enormous and extensive amounts of energy and investment being made in this space. It would be understandable if we were to think, given all of this attention and enthusiasm over the last several years, that companies have been making major leaps forward and realizing some significant benefits. However, the unfortunate truth is that the pervasiveness of Modernization and Transformation programs is not turning out to be a good thing for business. Not by a long shot. In fact, the results are trending in the exact opposite direction of the expected success and survival. While most companies have indeed been pursuing

Modernization and Transformation, banking on significant future value, the dark reality is this:

The vast majority of these initiatives are absolute failures.

The Numbers are Against Us

Failure, not success, has been the consistent theme for Modernization and Transformation efforts for many years now. For a company to successfully complete such an initiative is by far the exception to the rule, and the statistics supporting that assessment are glaringly consistent. Everest Group research says as much as 78% of these programs will fall short of their objectives or fail outright[3]. McKinsey & Company says 70% will fail[4]. Global research from Advanced shows 74% of legacy Modernization projects were started but never completed[5]. In fact, looking through all of the various industry reviews over the last several years there is a consistent trend of 70-80% failure rates for Modernization and Transformation initiatives, meaning approximately 3 out of 4 programs provide little to no return on their investment. This continuing trend of failure translates to absolutely massive losses for these companies.

The amount of annual funding and investment that has been poured into these efforts is enormous. In 2019, for example, the Harvard Business Review reported an estimated $1.3 trillion was spent on Digital Transformation initiatives. Yet most of those investments (around $900 billion) were wasted because 70% of those companies failed to achieve their Digital Transformation goals[6]. Look at that number again:

$900 *BILLION* - $900,000,000,000.00 - *WASTED.*

As a combined group the business leaders of these companies could be considered certifiably insane because so much money is frequently being thrown away consistently and publicly. There are no big cover ups happening here, as the numbers and the results are easy to find, and the numbers continue to rise. The International Data Corporation (IDC) predicts that global spending on the necessary technologies and services for digital transformation will reach $2.3 trillion by 2023[7]. With this being the current trend, it is as if it has become something of a cultural norm to accept the fact that these programs have and will continue to fail. Why is it that more and more companies are choosing to launch their own Modernization and Transformation initiatives? Why do those companies that have already suffered these kinds of losses continue to press on? It does not make logical nor financial sense that massive failures of this kind have become normalized and accepted to the point that they continue to happen in nearly every company. For those companies that have already gone down this path unsuccessfully, what is it that has continued to go so consistently wrong? Why do Board Members, CEOs, CIOs, CFOs, and other decision makers repeatedly choose to pay for all of this when there is such low probability for success? There seems to be something at play here that could be equated to our evolutionary and instinctual drive to 'Adapt or Die'. There is something that makes future survival and success seem worth these kinds of repeated attempts and failures. When survival is at stake, giving in to failure is simply not an option. The goal must be achieved at all costs. On one hand, we have become enamored with the image of a bright and prosperous future, while on the other, we are deathly afraid of the potential for a future in which that bright image is not realized, and we then become extinct.

That image of a brighter future is what spurs us on and moves us forward. It underlies the fact that the business cases being made for all of these Modernization and Transformation initiatives somehow remain compelling. If they weren't sufficiently convincing, then this amount of investment would be routed elsewhere given the abnormally high risk of failure. Yet true success continues to be stubbornly and consistently elusive. What organizations are faced with is a highly complex problem that is begging to be solved. The world, the market, customers, and business partners will continue to change and raise expectations – whether their companies are able to keep up or not. Said differently, the threat of *not* taking on a Modernization or Transformation initiative can be just as convincing as a well thought out business case in favor of the program. Regardless of the individual motivators, what is readily apparent is that the typical approaches being used in the multitude of attempts at Modernization and Transformation are severely lacking in what is actually needed to achieve important objectives. Failure is rampant. There are clearly pieces missing from this puzzle that are keeping organizations from putting it all together and achieving the intended outcomes that are absolutely necessary to succeed. Luckily, and as the study of evolution tells us, it has become a well-developed part of our nature to solve difficult puzzles in order to survive.

We Can't Resist a Good Puzzle

As human beings we are natural problem solvers. Different types of puzzles present themselves to us continuously in a variety of ways, and we enjoy trying to solve these puzzles because our brains have become fine-tuned for it over time. The definition of *Problem Solving* is this:

> *"the cognitive process of searching for a solution to a given problem or a path to reach a given goal"*

That cognitive process has been refined and deeply ingrained in us ever since the first modern humans started moving out of Africa nearly 100,000 years ago. Being good at solving puzzles has allowed us to continually adapt and survive. In today's business world, overcoming the problem of how to make a Modernization or Transformation successful is in effect a new type of highly challenging puzzle to be tackled. An organization must find the right path that allows them to reach the intended goal.

Even though solving problems is something we are all doing almost constantly on a small scale without even realizing it, like picking out matching clothes to wear for the day, encountering a more prominent and challenging problem is something that directly captures our attention and draws us in. Once presented with such a puzzle, it is amazingly difficult to leave it undone, which perhaps is yet another reason that companies continue to allocate substantial funding for their Modernization and Transformation initiatives. We can't help but submit to the gravitational pull of a complex problem begging to be solved that promises such satisfaction at its conclusion. The reason we feel this almost palpable need to solve these types of challenging puzzles and reach our goals is because that feeling is actually deeply rooted in the physical structure of our brains. Working on puzzles fully exercises both sides of our brains. The left-brain logical side is used in rationally identifying and fitting pieces together while the right-brain creative side envisions the big picture waiting at the end of the completed work. Working on a puzzle brings all of our mental capacities to bear and we revel in the challenge because it is exactly what our brains have been crafted for over millennia. Given the rate of failure, trying to solve the problem of Modernization or Transformation is clearly one of the most challenging puzzles we have in business today.

The problem-solving that goes into planning and undertaking a Modernization or Transformation initiative takes the same type of whole-brain approach. It requires both *creative thinking*, i.e., the strategy that defines the endgame, as well as *logical thinking*, i.e. the tactics and incremental steps to get you there. Therefore, knowing our evolutionary history and why we become so engaged in problem solving, it is all too easy for us to become enthusiastic about such an endeavor. This provides yet more understanding as to why it has been fairly easy to sell the ideas, get buy-in for the business cases and obtain the required funding for such large and complex programs – regardless of the high risk of failure. Yet lighting up both halves of our brains to solve this type of puzzle is only one half of the story. Once we've tapped into our problem-solving nature, we must also be able to perpetuate that enthusiasm and engagement throughout the entire initiative to effectively reduce the risk of failure. Luckily, we just happen to be built for that too.

Another reason so many of us enjoy doing puzzles is that the activity of working on a puzzle is directly tied to the goal-seeking behavior of our conscious mind, and this goal-seeking behavior in our mind also has a direct link to our physical body. Within us there is a chemical feedback loop built into our brain that keeps us wanting and striving for more. For example, when we are working on a jigsaw puzzle each piece we find and put into place gives us a little hit of dopamine which continues to build and build, piece by piece, until it culminates and climaxes at the puzzle's completion. You are mentally and physically (chemically) engaged in the process the entire time. This is also an extremely satisfying progression because during assembly you get to see and feel the progress you are making all the while knowing that you are working toward something bigger than what exists in the separated individual pieces. The experience is inherently more satisfying than the feeling you get when working to complete repetitive tasks on your mundane daily 'to-do' list. Solving a puzzle with enthusiasm is about doing something more gratifying, more meaningful. An effective approach to

Modernization and Transformation will leverage this progressive goal seeking behavior by crafting an incremental plan that steadily builds and works toward the final objectives.

If we can approach a Modernization or Transformation initiative through the lens of our natural abilities for problem solving and perpetuate it through our affinity for completing puzzles incrementally, then perhaps we can put ourselves back on track to finally realizing the truly meaningful and valuable outcomes that have been envisioned. But before jumping to exactly how we plan to go about solving the puzzle, we need to ensure that we are selecting a puzzle for ourselves that we are actually capable of solving in the first place. We need to pick a puzzle that solves specific problems in terms of our current context and capabilities. Knowing that the term 'Digital Transformation' can have wildly varying interpretations and definitions, being able to clearly articulate the desired outcomes and the intended future state will tell the entire organization exactly what puzzle is being selected to be pieced together and completed. Being mindful of certain critical details that need addressing during that 'selection' process is the first step toward achieving the success and survival we are seeking.

Choosing the Right Puzzle

There are very few people that can walk by someone working a puzzle and not get drawn in. For those that do get drawn in, if they find the puzzle too complex or too hard for them, they quickly become frustrated, give up and walk away. Those who are engaged in a Modernization or Transformation initiative react similarly. If it is too difficult for the people working on it, because they haven't yet developed the skills needed, or there are complexities they haven't yet grasped, the puzzle will never be finished; the problem never solved. If these struggles and challenges are not overcome in a timely manner, the continued survival of the organization may eventually come into question. Therefore, choosing the right puzzle at the right time for the right team is critical to achieving a positive outcome.

As human beings we perform best when we have tasks that we can not only complete successfully, but that challenge us *just enough* to engender feelings of accomplishment and satisfaction in the end. Throwing down a high-difficulty 5000-piece jigsaw puzzle in front of a group of 5-year-old children and expecting them to succeed at putting it together for you would most likely have a negative outcome. Not only have you set them up for failure by choosing an inappropriate puzzle for them, but they may be so disillusioned by the experience itself that they will shy away from the next puzzle they encounter. It is best to give them something they can accomplish and learn from, and then increase the difficulty and complexity progressively from there. Using an evolutionary and developmental approach such as this for Modernization and Transformation becomes of paramount importance when determining what exactly constitutes the 'right' puzzle for the organization at the current time.

Think about how many different things we take into consideration when we walk into a store to buy a jigsaw puzzle. We have to think about the age and capability of the people that will be working on the puzzle, determine what our acceptable price range is, and decide on the level of quality we expect from the selected product. Yet the biggest driver for most of us is what's on the front of the box - the picture of what the puzzle will look like when it is completed. We instinctively search for an image that we will enjoy assembling – especially if we think we will be working on it for an extended period of time. For some people, the completed project may even be something they plan to preserve or hang up on the wall to display when finished. This becomes an outward sign of perseverance and accomplishment. While some jigsaw puzzle aficionados may be looking for results that could be considered "Instagram-worthy", solving the puzzles of Modernization and Transformation initiatives could similarly be considered resume-building and profile-worthy for executives and IT professionals. For anyone looking forward to both achieving the program objectives and also highlighting their successes, it becomes doubly important to perform the due diligence necessary to 'pick the right puzzle' by defining clear goals, intentions, and guardrails before making any commitments. It would not be wise to build up hype around a picture of the desired result only to have a big hole of unfinished work right in the middle of it.

A Picture That Catches the Eye

By pointing out that the primary driver in puzzle selection is usually the picture or image of the final product, we are saying that we need to know the exact problem we are trying to solve before we actually get started. We also must have an image of what it will look like when the project is done because that picture of the future will help guide our actions along the way. In any Modernization or Transformation effort it is essential to be able to clearly articulate the goals and expected outcomes in a way that will orient all of the players and team members around common objectives. When taking time to think about specific drivers and objectives for a Modernization or Transformation effort, a representative 'image' or vision of the future must be created.

As mentioned earlier, one of the key problems across industries today is that the terms Modernization and Transformation can have wildly different definitions and interpretations from person to person and from company to company. Tack on any additional terms such as 'Digital', 'DevOps', 'Organizational', 'Cultural', or 'Agile' and we often get even less clarity as to what those programs truly entail. Regardless of what term is being applied to your particular initiative, you have to be able to expand on the topic coherently to create a clear picture for those who are on the receiving end of your message and direction. Your vision must be clear – the image distinct. For that, one of the best places to start is to capture and state what gave rise to the initiative in the first place – the underlying business drivers. Being able to clearly articulate the "Why" that led to the program itself can provide a sense of purpose that everyone can rally around. The specific drivers and purpose may differ greatly depending on whether the intention is to Modernize or to Transform the organization.

When looking at Modernization initiatives specifically, the drivers typically originate from some form of business progress being impeded by existing or aging technology. The current technology is, in effect, one of the main barriers to achieving further growth and progress for the company overall. Some examples of Modernization objectives are to:

- Provide new/better/faster products and services to customers.
- Lower the development and maintenance costs of technology assets.
- Increase data visibility, security, and analytical capabilities.
- Speed up partner onboarding and application integrations.
- Achieve compliance and be able to consistently meet SLAs.

- Establish real-time visibility into key metrics (cash flow, customer trends, system health, etc.)
- Improve management and control of existing applications and infrastructure.

Expanding the list to include common Transformation initiatives we can add:

- Integrating technology into all business areas.
- Moving to new business and/or operational models.
- Changing how value is delivered to customers and/or moving to a customer-centric approach.
- Cultural, Leadership, DevOps, Organizational, and/or Agile oriented Transformations.
- Process Automation to Reduce Manual Overhead.
- Implementing Advanced Data Analytics, Machine Learning, Artificial Intelligence, and the like.
- Physical working environment changes such as open floor plans, remote working, or an expanding regional/global workforce.

Although this list could be considered as only scratching the surface of all possibilities, it serves to highlight why there can be so much confusion and misunderstanding when using the generic terms of Modernization and Transformation to describe such a wide variety of undertakings. When we think of the rate of failure across all of these initiatives, much of that can be traced back to being unclear or vague rather than absolutely explicit in conveying the drivers, the intent, and the expected outcomes, as well as not communicating those things clearly and often over the course of the program.

If you are considering a new initiative, or if your program is already underway, before going any further see if you can state exactly what value you are trying to realize and why. This can be any combination of business value and/or value to the customer. Then consider if the same information has been or will be explicitly communicated to all of the stakeholders *and* participants of the program. The reason for going through this exercise is to ensure there is adequate transparency regarding the existing problems and barriers that need to be solved for. You are then able to create a sense of common purpose and alignment. By sharing the information broadly and inviting commentary and feedback, it helps to validate that the problems themselves actually exist as you currently understand them, which in turn facilitates broader buy-in and support. Including information that also addresses the costs of *not* Modernizing or Transforming can also create a sense of urgency. Highlighting the specific opportunities that exist and/or the goals to be achieved creates a mental image of the future for everyone involved. Painting a crystal-clear picture in people's minds of what your intended future looks like becomes the touchstone and reference point that can be used throughout the program. It becomes the singular image that people will identify with and look forward to achieving.

One final consideration regarding this point is that to successfully rally people around a common purpose, they have to actually *like* the vision of the future you are creating for them. Ideally you are sharing an image that, when completed, will make your customers happy, the business happy, employees happy, *and* make you happy. Communicating that effectively gives each individual several options in which to find some positive motivation. That personal incentive is the key to increased engagement simply because solving a puzzle with a picture we like makes us happy. It's why we choose to work on puzzles in the first place.

What Quality Looks Like

Picture yourself coming across a puzzle with a picture on the box that is one of the most impressive that you have ever seen. You buy it and take it home with a real sense of anticipation. Once you get there you eagerly open the box and get to work only to realize that the puzzle itself is a complete piece of junk. The high-quality version of the image on the box lid has turned grainy and unclear, the pieces are not cut cleanly, peel apart easily, and some of the pieces are warped. The connections are loose and difficult to work with because they don't provide a tight fit. There seems to be nothing right with it. This is not what you expected at all. What started out as a great and highly anticipated endeavor has turned into the disappointing reality of something destined for the garbage bin.

In any undertaking, a lack of quality can very quickly turn excitement and enthusiasm created by the initial vision into disdain and disillusionment when, in actuality, it turns out to be a shoddy and underwhelming representation. This is true whether the final product is an assembled picture puzzle or the future state you intend to create through your Modernization or Transformation initiative. Knowing and precisely defining what constitutes 'quality' is a critical underlying aspect that will determine if your vision is, and will continue to be seen as, something worth pursuing. Once you have sketched out a fairly good representation of what the final picture is going to look like, the level of quality that you find acceptable and aesthetically pleasing could make or break the perceived success of your program. For these types of initiatives and investments, quality is not something you can leave to the cliché 'I'll know it when I see it'. Setting expectations for quality is the difference between having a clear image or a grainy one. It is the difference between having solid, well-built pieces and those that peel apart and tear away with use. It is the difference behind being able to identify reputable and trustworthy participants, vendors, and suppliers versus ending up with those only looking to make a quick buck with shoddy products and services. Quality cannot be deferred to a later date due to the exponential level of risk that grows over time when there is no clear picture of what quality looks like.

Depending on the specific drivers and objectives laid out in your vision, quality can be defined both quantitatively and qualitatively. There may be specific numbers and measurements that Modernization or Transformation is intended to influence. There may also be specific behavioral or cultural changes to be achieved. In all likelihood, an initiative will be successful only by realizing some combination of the two types of quality objectives. Knowing if your intermediate and incremental changes are having the intended results will also require a combination of leading and lagging indicators across all aspects of the program. You need to know what signposts to look for along the journey that tell you that you are on the right track. You have to know that the pieces that are being put in place are in the right spots. Otherwise, subsequent pieces placed will be leading you further away from your goal. We will not go into further details just yet, as specific types of quality measurements will be presented in more detail later during the discussion on Developmental Lines. Our attention now turns to leveraging a clear high-quality picture with those who will most need to sustain the excitement and enthusiasm throughout the program, being the team members themselves.

An Appropriate Level of Difficulty

Recalling the earlier example of telling a group of 5-year-old children to assemble a highly difficult 5000-piece jigsaw puzzle, we can easily identify the high probability that they will not come anywhere close to successfully completing the task. Balancing a Modernization or Transformation vision with an appropriate level of difficulty for the people involved is something that must be directly addressed to help reduce the risk to the program. Not managing this balancing act as an ongoing risk has consistently come back to haunt those that have ignored or lightly brushed over this specific dynamic during their initiatives.

The level of difficulty and complexity of Modernization and Transformation initiatives has too often been grossly underestimated during planning. When a better understanding and realization of the challenges at hand emerges, it is common that these complexities and difficulties are minimized and discounted throughout the remainder of the program. Few people are willing or empowered to openly report that an effort of this importance and magnitude has gone off course or that the goals might be inappropriate based on the struggles people encounter along the way.

Part of this recurring underestimation and understatement of a program's complexity can be attributed to a lack of explicit consideration of the current capabilities of the people throughout the organization at the start of the initiative. The focus during strategy definition is often, by default, more heavily consumed with visions of the future state, the 'what is to be', and the new technologies and 'shiny objects' that get to be played with and put in place as part of the program. Enamored with what awaits us at the finish line we forget to consider those standing at the starting line and whether they can successfully navigate the entire course ahead of them. Therefore, during the planning stage we must address the inherent difficulties that exist around being able to change and evolve the mindsets and behaviors of those people, as we will be depending on them to perform to our expectations.

As the vision and approach for a Modernization or Transformation initiative is being finalized, there is very often an underlying assumption that if the staff is told what to do and given the relevant training, then they will (and must) be able to bring the vision of the program to life. There is rarely an approach defined that is intentionally based on incremental progress and evolutionary maturation of the teams and the individuals that make up those teams. While this might be the case for new products, processes, and technologies, it is consistently less so for the people themselves. The mandate for the teams has been to '*do*', not necessarily to '*become*'. Although unintentional, programs are put at risk before they ever begin when there is a lack of understanding of the human development required to go alongside the planned process and technology improvements.

The people who will be working on the initiative are only who they are in this moment. No more, no less. This means that each one of them has the potential to experience personal difficulty and discomfort when leadership pushes them to make the leap to the future state without considering all of who they are, how they think and what they believe. For many initiatives, the 'people' part of the equation is reduced to providing them with requisite job skills, not the requisite state of being. The failure rate of Modernization and Transformation initiatives may itself tell us this is not working, but it can directly be seen when researching reasons why these programs continue to struggle. Per the most recent annual report published by digital.ai[8], three of the top four challenges experienced when adopting new ways of working were:

- General Organization Resistance to Change
- Not Enough Leadership Participation
- Organizational Culture at Odds with Proposed Values

These all speak to the current state of the individuals and teams themselves. These are human behavior reasons that exist independently of the program objectives. Personal habits, beliefs, understanding, and openness to change are all top contributors to whether or not a program will be successful. When the vision for Modernization or Transformation has been built around what is 'right' for the business, but not necessarily adding to that what is 'right' for the people that make up that organization, we can see the impact of neglecting to identify an appropriate level of difficulty and then managing it accordingly. For many failed initiatives, the plan and approach were too challenging for people to achieve relative to the defined objectives and vision. It was out of balance from the start.

As we noted earlier, people perform best when they have tasks at which they are competent and in which they can succeed but that challenge them ***just enough*** to feel accomplished when completed. If you choose something too easy you run the risk of disinterest, lack of engagement and forfeiting any meaningful change. Be overly aggressive by selecting something that is too hard to achieve, and you might see disillusionment, disengagement or even 'transformation theater', i.e., outward facing superficial changes in words and actions without any true changes to underlying maturity or tangible improvements. Therefore, consideration and attention must be given to this crucial balancing act of determining what is both challenging *and* achievable. Once that balance point has been identified, it inherently provides a reality check on whether the current state of the vision is indeed a readily achievable goal that maximizes performance. If not, there must be a change made to the goals and expectations that target a first-order or incremental change milestone. Pulling back from a more grandiose vision to an objective of appropriate difficulty allows for incremental and evolutionary growth of the people involved without being too complex and overwhelming for them. Being able to achieve some initial objectives that excite and engage the teams will in turn enable their own further growth and maturity as time passes. This allows them to readily engage with even more complex and difficult objectives as time goes on. The end result may be an initial Modernization or Transformation program that is whole unto itself but also a part of a longer-term evolutionary strategy. A puzzle within a puzzle if you will. Perhaps even one that establishes a new norm of continuous improvement and reinvention that reduces the need for more large-scale and costly initiatives in the future.

Consider the Workspace

There is one last consideration to discuss that, if ignored or forgotten during initial planning, can accelerate failure in a Modernization or Transformation initiative. The environment in which the program work will be performed can be just as important as the program being worked on within that environment. Imagine that you purchased a jigsaw puzzle with a picture of something that was very meaningful to you, and also met your requirements precisely in terms of being of good quality with the right level of difficulty. Finding what seemed to be an ideal fit made you excited to buy it and rush home to get working on it. Yet it wasn't' until you arrived there to begin putting it together that you realized the puzzle was so big that you didn't own a table large enough to handle the job. You believed that you had taken everything into account when picking out just the right puzzle, and yet the whole endeavor still turned out to be a resounding failure. The scenario could have been avoided consideration had been given not only the image, quality, complexity, and difficulty of the product, but *also* to the workspace and tools needed to get the job done. A project cannot be completed if there is not an appropriate environment in which to work. The environments in which Modernization and Transformation initiatives will be developed and refined is a key condition that contributes to the overall chances of program success. For a work environment to be considered complete, it must contain many different components, each of which warrants special attention.

Physical locations may be the most easily and readily recognized component of a work environment that needs to be examined, such as sufficient office space to accommodate the different needs of individuals and teams. Being able to dedicate space for individual work as well as collaborative space, such as a 'Caves & Commons' approach to office space set up, has been proven to directly contribute to high performing teams and overall program success. A balance of quiet private locations as well as shared spaces built with collaboration in mind can facilitate the various types of work that occur throughout a program. The physical environment created for the teams has a direct correlation to the speed and effectiveness of information transfer and overall program productivity.

Yet working environments inside of actual office buildings may not always be necessary or even financially sound choices in today's highly connected world. With the advent of work from home and hybrid remote-office models, the actual environment that needs to be addressed may be more clearly defined by the tools and accessories required to do the work itself along with ways for people to connect virtually. It is this group of tools and accessories that will be utilized and employed by the people working on the program that will equip them to ultimately realize the final vision and objectives.

In a similar manner to searching for an appropriate level of difficulty, there must also be an assessment of the tools currently being used to determine if specific short-term goals must be defined for upgrading, enhancing, expanding or replacing the tool sets themselves. Depending on the technologies being considered in the future vision, there may be a certain need to change out or introduce new software packages, connectivity capabilities, hardware, software development languages, service providers and vendors, or any number of things that are prerequisites before the teams can even begin their actual Modernization or Transformation work. This is precisely where the typical focus mentioned earlier, i.e., telling people what to do and giving them the requisite training, comes into play. You can give them the tools and the training, but that is only *part* of what needs to be considered. If you *don't* do a conscious assessment and prepare the team with the needed tools and training, you are only *increasing* the risk of a program failure.

That said, the tools and working environment are rarely, if ever, an outright oversight in planning for these programs. It is, however, still warranted to call it out as a key consideration for the sake of completeness. The entire environment in which people will be working, both physically and technically, needs to be examined for limiting factors and inhibitors to achieving the vision. For now, we are simply noting that the workspace is a consideration that needs to be addressed during planning and preparation for a Modernization or Transformation program. This topic will be explored in more detail later as part of the discussion regarding Mapping the Current State.

To create a holistic view of the current state, the vision, and the path to get from here to there demands taking into consideration all of the aspects discussed in this chapter. Once the exercise of choosing a vision/image has been completed, and clarity on quality, difficulty and environmental factors has been achieved, the next step is to start laying out all of the individual pieces to your puzzle. It is time to begin the difficult work of putting the thing together piece by piece. Of course, there is a glaring assumption at this point that we actually *have* all of the pieces we need...

Identifying All the Pieces

Picture yourself again with that new jigsaw puzzle that you're really excited about getting started on. You sit down, break open the seal on the box and then do exactly what you always do when you open a new puzzle - you dump out all the pieces in a big pile and start to work through them. You immediately start applying your usual methodic approach to getting the job done. You've done it so many times that it has become second nature to you. One by one you flip the pieces over, you align them, you group them – side pieces, corner pieces, colors, and patterns – laying everything out in front of you. You even come across a few pieces that can be placed together right away. You're caught up in the moment, highly focused, and enjoying it. Progress is clearly being made and it all just feels right. But is it?

Taking a well-known, comfortable, and familiar approach, such as the jigsaw puzzle example helps us to visualize, is exactly how most Modernization and Transformation efforts set themselves up for failure. When starting a large and complex program it often begins with an unfounded assumption that we know everything that needs to be done to achieve the objectives. This is a problem because we've assumed that we are working with *all* the pieces we need to solve the puzzle. While we rarely have to be concerned about this problem when doing an actual jigsaw puzzle, it is much more of a risk when dealing with a complex initiative. Yet companies continue to take the same methodic approach time after time working with complete trust that a tried-and-true methodology contains all the pieces and parts needed to complete the project. A 75% failure rate in Modernization and Transformation programs tells us that we are indeed missing some pieces, and perhaps several pieces, which we need to find before we can finish the puzzle in front of us.

Missing Pieces - The People, Process & Technology Fallacy

In the jigsaw puzzle analogy, there is a certain simplicity regarding the elements that come into play when doing that type of project. Normally a puzzle is chosen, the pieces are dumped on the table, it gets assembled piece by piece and - *'voila!'* – the final picture is complete. Those same aspects can be viewed in a similar manner when looking at a very common mantra spoken at one time or another during almost every Modernization and Transformation initiative. The 3-word mantra of **People, Process and Technology** encapsulates the belief that for the program to be truly successful all three of those elements must be equally addressed. To illustrate that point, the ***people*** working on a jigsaw puzzle will naturally and immediately fall into familiar approaches and roles, using the ***process*** they've previously learned and used to tackle the job at hand, and are typically working with a well-established knowledge of what a puzzle is, how pieces interlock, and where it is being put together (i.e., the ***technology***). The three aspects come together to enable the achievement of the goal. That straightforward approach seems like a sound foundational thought model that can be extrapolated out to larger and more complex initiatives. It seems to hit on everything a program needs to succeed, and also captures some of the 'gotchas' that have plagued past efforts. In fact, the People, Process & Technology (PPT) thought model has been used to help manage organizational change for more than 60 years. That kind of long track record has allowed PPT to deeply ingrain itself in our collective thinking. For most of that 60-year history the focus of the change programs has been on improving operational efficiency and optimizing various corporate functions. Today's initiatives are not that straightforward and uncomplicated in terms of the goals and objectives they are trying to achieve.

Over the last several years the three seemingly simple words of People, Process and Technology have been appropriated to describe the structure and totality of a wide variety of complex programs, including Modernization and Transformation initiatives. The thinking and approach are used so frequently that the term is virtually ubiquitous in business today. There is a widespread belief and assumption that this model provides a clear and comprehensive view to the elements that must be addressed in order to succeed. There are even formal frameworks and methods built around the People, Process & Technology approach, some of which have dubbed the three aspects as the "Golden Triangle". This visualization of a triangle is interesting because it leads us to continuously attempt to balance and counteract the impact of change in one aspect by adjusting the other two accordingly. People, Process and Technology, all in balance and working together will deliver success. On the surface it seems relatively uncomplicated and easy to understand. What else could there possibly be beyond those three aspects? Yet if we take an even slightly deeper look, we quickly realize that there is much more in play than what those three words might lead us to believe.

When something seems so straightforward and clear to us, it is easy for us to forget just how much goes into completing even the most mundane of tasks that we do every day. We are constantly solving problems and making decisions throughout every waking hour of every day. In fact, the average adult makes as many as 35,000 choices per day[9]. When making these choices, we incorporate everything we've learned and experienced over the course of our lives, including the unique ways that we think and interact, as well as the various skills we've built up along the way. The sum total of which highlights a reality that is actually quite far beyond the simplicity with which we normally label and describe what is needed to achieve a desired result or goal. Think about all of the things you had to accomplish when learning to walk, which was many years before even approaching the point of learning how to tie your shoes to put on those walking feet. Now all of that is taken for granted because putting on your shoes and walking to your destination has become second nature. All of the related struggles, frustrations and learning that got you there have been mostly, if not completely forgotten. For many years now Modernization and Transformation efforts have espoused that to achieve desired success the 'Big Three' critical components that need to be addressed are People, Process and Technology. It is a good label in its simplicity, but it does not adequately represent everything that goes into that label.

Business leaders and pundits are absolutely right to call out the importance of these 'Big Three' aspects of PPT in Modernization and Transformation initiatives because they all have a profound impact on one another as well as on the capability to realize an ultimate combined endgame. The problem lurking behind the use of this convenient and familiar tagline is that the terms themselves are so inescapably vague that they give no true direction or guidance. This is strikingly similar to the fact that a term like 'Digital Transformation' means so many different things to so many different people. The attention and approach given to each one of the PPT aspects can be cripplingly limited by the unique interpretation and experience of each person responsible for filling out the details that these words might point to. As those details are filled in, and those interpretations become strategies and tactics, the three 'aspects' of a complete program more often than not immediately turn into separate and distinct 'categories' of work.

When looking through this lens of distinction and separation, it is easier to see how each of the three categories is regularly expanded in relative isolation from the others. Each one starts to identify and contain multiple components, characteristics and sub-categories that can be added to the scope of a program. The category of "People" might contain training and reskilling employees, changing HR policies, defining career development paths, adjusting performance reviews, measuring productivity, and so on. The "Process" category could be addressing financial and budgeting structures, product and software development life cycles, customer interaction methods, or required legal and compliance procedures that must be followed. "Technology" work may originate from an internal enterprise architecture perspective, or external customer channels, or the tools employees need to do their jobs. In reality, the above examples across all three categories barely scratch the surface of everything that might, and often does, fall under those headers – and the specific mix of all of them is inherently unique to each organization. Obviously, the breadth and complexity of a Modernization or Transformation initiative can become exponentially large very quickly, which is why it is imperative to remain conscious of how easy it is to lose sight of the interconnectedness of the whole picture as we encounter more and more complexity. As complexity goes up, individual preferences and biases become more prominent[10], taking an initiative off course before you know it.

Research shows that even though plenty of lip service gets paid to the mantra of People, Process & Technology, individual initiatives frequently show a significantly skewed attention to only one of the three categories. This is typically driven by the person or group ultimately responsible for owning and delivering the program. For example, Information Technology, Enterprise Architecture and Software or Systems Development people are naturally drawn to the newest breakthroughs in technology. They enthusiastically pursue leading (or 'bleeding') edge technology in the name of staying up-to-date and proclaiming new tech as the means by which the company will stay competitive and profitable. Those thinking that a change in 'culture' is the key to unlocking next-level success will normally have a strong 'people' bias. They will lean towards the pursuit of human behavioral concepts like unlocking innovative thinking, becoming more flexible, nimble, and adaptive, improving attraction and retention of top talent, aligning around new values and mission statements, and similar topics. All of these are often rolled out with rhetoric that speaks to a collective 'transformation' that will allow the company to break free from the chains of the past and create a brighter future. Those with a proclivity for an already proven approach will tend to gravitate directly to the 'process' category. They often instinctively lean toward copying or emulating successes they have had in other organizations, or they try to implement the same processes, techniques and methodologies that are known to have worked well in other companies. Each of these types of situations are unintentionally, but nevertheless effectively, myopic.

When personal biases take hold, it leads a program away from the ability to ground and orient each sub-initiative in the context of a complete and balanced approach for the overall program. Those individuals that built the business case for their

Modernization or Transformation initiative may have said the right things about making the appropriate changes across People, Process & Technology when they were getting buy-in, funding and kicking off the program, but in reality, they had a significantly reduced chance of success because of their natural affinity for only one particular aspect. It is that gravitational pull of what is well-known and interesting to a particular individual or group that ends up moving them farther away from an approach that should be in balance with the other categories.

The research into why Modernization and Transformation initiatives fail has frequently attributed those failures to this subconscious movement away from a more balanced People, Process and Technology approach. Some researchers and pundits say that attention needs to be explicitly and equally balanced across all three elements, while others state that an increased amount of attention needs to be placed on one or two of the other categories that are different from our common biases toward a single aspect. Although the research is legion, there is no consistent theme other than commentary that always speaks to some form of breakdown in how each company has approached the three aspects of People, Process and Technology and the recommendations are always that some *other* combination of PPT is the way for companies to avoid a similar fate. Since this is effectively sending us in circles and leaving us stuck in a cycle of failure, we need to break free from this cycle by looking elsewhere for an appropriate epiphany.

It is true that an imbalance across People, Process and Technology is what has driven many programs to their demise, but failure due to a lack of balance is not the cause of each and every one of these documented program failures. Although this definitely applies to a large percentage of the initiatives, there are many companies that had what appeared to be a balanced approach and still ended up in the failure column. The root cause of such a high failure rate across all Modernization and Transformation initiatives is not so easily identified. There are yet more pieces that are still missing from this puzzle.

Shortcomings in one or more of the 'Big Three' aspects may indeed be why many Modernization and Transformation initiatives have failed. There is, however, another, an even more disconcerting problem behind declaring that a subconscious, myopic focus (or some other failing) around People, Process and Technology is the root cause of every one of these failures. Those programs, those failures and that research all assume that the People, Process & Technology approach in itself is a complete and comprehensive thought model. Although PPT addresses important and necessary aspects, it is in truth only *partial*, and must be augmented and extended if we want to increase the chances of success for Modernization and Transformation programs overall. The high failure rate points to the reality that our thinking in this space may not have evolved as much as we want to believe it has, nor has our approach revealed itself to be the complete and comprehensive one that we need to drive successful programs. A different approach is needed that includes *more* than what we have used in the past. As Albert Einstein said,

> *"We cannot solve our problems with the same thinking we used when we created them."*

We have created a problem that is wasting nearly *one trillion dollars* a year by using the People, Process and Technology approach repeatedly in the same generic manner. Analyzing this problem through a different lens shows us that the various Modernization and Transformation initiatives that have typically oriented thinking around the standard People, Process and Technology approach has resulted in making specific changes in what can best be described as 'tangible' areas. PPT is very strong and mature when it comes to driving changes in policies, processes, tools, and technology. The root of what we see as the fallacy of PPT lies in the fact that these types of changes are all *EXTERNAL* to the people involved in, and impacted by, the effort. The "People" part of People, Process & Technology has effectively been reduced to what the people *DO*, not who they *ARE*. This reductionism results in leadership taking approaches that commonly focus on training and upskilling their people. This inadvertently dehumanizes the 'people' part of the equation, essentially discounting and rejecting what those people actually *THINK, FEEL AND BELIEVE*. This is an absolutely crucial aspect of Modernization and Transformation programs that often goes unaddressed. It can also be the most difficult aspect to manage effectively because dealing with what is *inside* of people is messy and inherently difficult to quantify. People think for themselves and every individual brings their own perspectives, inclinations, and beliefs into the equation. Affecting change in an organization verifiably is not as straightforward and methodical as companies have believed it to be. By not addressing this additional aspect of change, most of their initiatives continue to result in failure. This highlights that a much higher level of complexity exists around today's Modernization and Transformation initiatives that must be dealt with. While PPT does a wonderful job of addressing what is external to the organization's people, consideration must also be given to what is *INTERNAL* to generate some form of balanced and comprehensive strategy that will allow a program to complete the picture and realize the objective. It is these internal aspects that are the key to expanding our thinking on how to drive organizational development and maturity as a whole.

All told, as Modernization and Transformation initiatives continue looking to meet their objectives through the lens of People, Process & Technology the results are akin to trying to do a jigsaw puzzle that is missing several pieces. If you knew at the outset that your puzzle didn't have all of the pieces, you wouldn't even attempt to put it together, much less shell out the money for it. Simply put, a puzzle cannot be considered complete unless you have ALL THE PIECES and those pieces have been interlocked and joined together at the same time to create the final image. What we need is to both include and transcend the important but partial mindset of People, Process

& Technology, and allow ourselves to evolve to the next level of thinking and problem solving. The task at hand is to identify what truly is the entire set of pieces needed to make the entire puzzle fit together as a unified and cohesive whole.

Finding Pieces - The Four Corners

If we are to go beyond the People, Process & Technology model while not losing sight of the value it provides, we need to look at PPT from a different perspective and vantage point[11]. We can start by explicitly acknowledging that all of the aspects, dynamics and characteristics of any organization have both *interior (subjective)* and *exterior (objective)* components that combine to create an overall picture of reality. As human beings, the interior and exterior halves of our existence are inextricably intertwined, and this applies equally in a business context. Our minds, thoughts, and emotions, both individually and collectively, play as much a part in our work lives (if not more) as do the physical and tangible things we interact with to do our work. Everything comes together in order to provide value to customers and the business. The way people interpret, experience, and feel about things (*the interior*) ends up being just as relevant to success as those things in their environment that they can touch, see, and hear throughout the organization (*the exterior*).

Where the previous discussion uncovered the outward-facing tendencies when using the three-aspect People, Process & Technology thought model, we are now compelled to address the resulting realization that the internal half of the 'People' part of the equation demands equal attention in order to establish a more balanced and comprehensive approach. That realization can be restated by saying that change initiatives such as Modernization and Transformation programs must address both interior *and* exterior aspects for everyone involved in and impacted by the program. 'Interior' in this case refers to the subjective aspects of thoughts, beliefs, inclinations, and the like, while 'Exterior' refers to the objective and environmental aspects such as the skill sets, tools, techniques, policies, and organizational structures that are normally included in the People, Process & Technology model.

For this perspective to provide a complete view and representation of the organization being changed, both interior and exterior considerations must be applied at both an individual level and a collective level. The individual level addresses each person both internally and externally, while the collective addresses anything that applies to groups of people such as teams, departments, or the organization structure and operations overall. There is no transformation without people, so it is critical for the interiors to be considered just as important as the exteriors.

It is often stated and understood that in order to be successful you must capture people's hearts and minds, but it is with much less regularity that an initiative defines how to accomplish that objective as an explicit part of the overall program plan. By taking this perspective of approaching a Modernization or Transformation initiative with the intent to address both interior and exterior aspects, as well as individual and collective aspects, we have inherently incorporated the 'hearts and minds' sentiment. What we have uncovered is the basis for an extended four-aspect thought model that goes beyond the three-aspect PPT model. These four aspects can be viewed and described as:

- Personal – the individual interior aspect
- Cultural – the collective interior aspect
- Employment – the individual exterior aspect
- Organizational – the collective exterior aspect

These four aspects can also be diagrammatically depicted as quadrants:

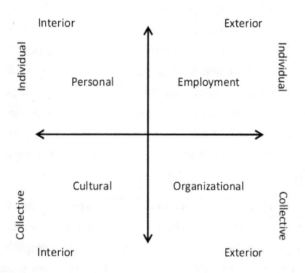

This expanded thought model can be used to visualize a unified and comprehensive Modernization or Transformation initiative, while emphasizing that there are four contributing aspects that make up such an effort. This model can also be utilized as a lens through which to examine both the current state of the company as well as the image of the future that the initiative is intending to realize. By considering and addressing both the whole and its integral parts, it is more likely that the risk of having an incomplete or biased approach will decrease while the overall chances for program success will increase accordingly. This is primarily because when looking at these four aspects, both individually and in total, it provides a framework through which to identify a more comprehensive set of insights regarding where the organization currently stands and where it needs to go. They are the four dimensions of the problem to be solved. This expanded set of elements becomes the four corners that define the outer boundaries of the puzzle.

That all said, below is a brief overview that provides a few more details regarding what each of these quadrants (i.e., aspects) represent. Complete details on their contents and how to use them to capture and communicate specifics will be discussed in subsequent sections. For now, it is sufficient to see these quadrants as the categories within which we will be able to group specific types of puzzle pieces that will then be pieced together to create a complete image.

Organizational – Collective Environments

The Organizational quadrant in the lower right of the four-aspect model is where most companies put their initial focus when discussing how to go about a Modernization and

Transformation initiative. This quadrant represents the processes, tools, technologies, and organizational structures that characterize the entire organization, how it operates, its component parts, and the actual products and services it provides to customers. As all of these pieces are 'empirical' in that they can be directly observed in some form or fashion, they represent the Collective Exterior (Objective) aspect of the organization. This is the organizational ecosystem in which everything else exists and operates.

The Organizational quadrant embodies the social structures, governance practices and overall environment of the company. It can be described as an 'inter-objective reality', being the common world of experience shared by all groups of people and entities throughout the company. It is also useful to note that this quadrant also contains any legal and compliance aspects that apply to many companies, such as healthcare, government, and financial institutions, as those are very much an integral part of the organizational environment and have significant influence on many other aspects.

It is in the contents of this quadrant where Modernization and Transformation efforts seek to change, develop, and mature things like the enterprise technology and architecture, organizational models, Human Resources policies, reward and compensation structures, financial management and reporting requirements, strategic plans, company vision/mission/value statements, business processes and life cycles, and both internal and external communications. The Organizational environment contains the pieces that are the easiest to see, and therefore over which it is easiest to feel some sense of control.

Employment – Individual Environments

The Employment quadrant in the upper right of the model represents the processes, tools, and technologies that any given individual employee will use (employ) to successfully do their job on a day-to-day basis. As these are all things that are 'observable and outside' of an employee themselves, this quadrant is the Individual Exterior (Objective) aspect that defines a particular employee's environment. This in effect corresponds to a subset of the overall collective environment of the Organizational quadrant described above.

The Employment quadrant is where companies leverage specialized processes, tools and technologies that are relevant to only a specific group of people that perform work for the organization. For example, IT applications people may be working with approved software development languages or environments, certain code management tools and techniques, and possibly waterfall or Agile delivery methods. Sales and Marketing personnel may be working with specific customer or demographic databases, tools for campaigns or customer relationship management (CRM), company commission structures, and standardized order entry processes. Regardless of the particular employee role, there are exterior behaviors, actions and movements that are expected of them. The Employment quadrant exemplifies how the environment is created and maintained so that those expectations can be adequately met by each individual. Each individual needs the tools and rules required to get the job done the way the company wants it done.

Cultural -Team Dynamics

Now we move to the more nebulous 'interior' left-hand side of the four-quadrant model. The Cultural quadrant at the lower left represents any shared values, feelings, beliefs, attitudes, behaviors, language, and relationships that exist throughout the organization. Culture may not be something that can be seen or touched in any physical form, but we definitely experience it and know what it is at every company we enter. The interpersonal and relationship dynamics that create what we call 'culture' can be particular to specific teams or groups within an organization or apply to the entire organization as 'one team'. We experience 'culture' in the way people interact with one another, and that may change depending on who is participating in specific interactions and in different contexts. These observable interactions stem from the collective values that are held within the organization which also drive the decisions being made. The values we are referring to here are those that are believed and understood, which may or may not align with the values that the organization communicates publicly, or merely aspires to. This is the quadrant that describes the cultural reality.

The Culture aspect seeks to capture the overall experience of 'we' that comes from being part of a group of people. What we define as culture is a unique intersubjective conception held by a group of individuals. More often than not we try to describe company culture in terms of attitudes or general behaviors. For example, 'leadership' may be characterized as 'command and control', or a company may be known for being 'customer-centric' in their approach to all aspects of their business. This is also the quadrant that captures the attitudes of the employees relative to their employer where we might have positive descriptors such as 'casual', 'inclusive', 'nimble' or 'progressive', or less flattering reviews such as 'toxic', 'siloed', 'outdated' or 'stressful'. The key with this quadrant is to capture the collective feeling of the organization or group as opposed to what may be a particular individual's assessment.

The Culture quadrant can also be expanded beyond an organization's borders to include customers, partners, and vendors as they all can sense and influence the collective experience of the company itself. Adding representation for groups outside of the company in this model can be viewed as a recognition of a broader 'we' that may also directly influence how to approach a Modernization or Transformation initiative. The reason being that the perceptions of those groups, including their own interior values, beliefs, behaviors, language, and relationships, may carry significant weight in the business strategy that the company is looking to pursue.

The Cultural quadrant described here, and the Personal quadrant in the next section, are an elaboration on the People, Process & Technology fallacy discussed in the prior chapter. Thinking of the People aspect of PPT in terms of what people 'do' in effect discounts the Cultural and Personal quadrants that are used in this model. When devising a Modernization or Transformation plan that addresses people in the organization as 'they' instead of 'we' it ends up as an impersonal and objective approach that is better aligned with this model's lower-right Organizational quadrant. In the impersonal approach often seen in PPT, the people have been reduced to being scientifically observable, measurable, and capable of being manipulated and molded into what the planners believe they should be. For those who have gone through an impersonal 'just train the teams' type of approach in the past, they have learned the hard way that Culture itself demands otherwise because people are more than tools to be employed to achieve a goal.

Personal – Individual Dynamics
The fourth and final quadrant is the most diverse and wide ranging in both actuality and potential. The Personal dynamic, representing what particular individuals think, feel, and believe about their job and their employer, is in no way consistent from person to person. Their entire personal history, belief system, preferences, goals, and desires – and in many cases personal challenges – will create a completely unique perspective, definition, and interpretation of their work life. That said, this quadrant comprises the Individual Interior (Subjective) aspect, which is the inward personal nature as well as the outward facing personas one brings to work every day. It is inherently the most difficult aspect to consider and influence in a Modernization and Transformation program because it becomes more and more

complex and wide-ranging as the number of individuals in the company increases.

Although challenging, including the Personal quadrant explicitly when both planning the program as well as capturing and describing the state of the organization provides a solid foundation from which to build a much more grounded and pragmatic approach. Much of what constitutes a successful Modernization or Transformation effort comes from changing and establishing human behaviors. The more we know about what is going on inside of people's heads, the better chance we have of understanding their current behaviors, how to overcome them, and shift to desired behaviors that will enable the achievement of the overall objectives.

Interlocking Aspects – Pieces of Pieces

For those following along closely you may have noticed what seems to be an issue with the description of this four-quadrant model. How will this visualization method capture the different characteristics of every individual, every team, every process, and the entire organization itself? If you're thinking that there is no way to visualize that effectively in four quadrants on a single diagram then you are absolutely right.

To address this, we need to introduce the concept of a holon. The word 'holon' is Greek for whole/parts, meaning literally that the whole is simultaneously a part and vice versa. To illustrate the concept, consider the following progression of matter:

- Quarks

- Atoms

- Molecules

- Cells

- Organisms

- Communities

- Societies

Although from a strict scientific point of view there are a few other entities between some of those items listed, the point is that each one of them is both a whole entity unto itself and also an integral and constituent part of the next higher order item. If you were to remove all of the instances of a particular item on the list, all of the higher order items would cease to exist, but not the lower order items. For example, molecules could still exist if there were no cells or organisms but take away all the atoms and you lose all the molecules as well as everything else up the chain. Each item in this list is therefore a holon that can be both a whole unit as well as a fundamental part of something more significant and complex.

For the four-quadrant model above, a single instance of the quadrant diagram can be used to describe any of the given 'holons' in our organization, such as a particular individual, a particular team, a particular environmental component (process, tool, technology, etc.), or the organization as a whole. For example, if we were creating a diagram to represent the entire organization, the Cultural quadrant at the organizational level would be an averaged representation of all of the teams in the company, while each team themselves would have their own diagrammatic representation that is embedded within that quadrant. The same holds true for the Employment quadrant, both of which are seen in the visual representation below:

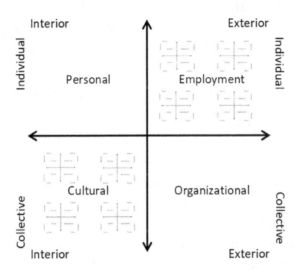

This in effect provides the capability of generating a nested model of four-quadrant diagrams that can capture all of the various characteristics and entities that need to be considered in a Modernization and Transformation initiative. This nested approach can address multiple layers of depth as, for example, there may be teams that exist within a 'team of teams' which may be part of a particular department (another form of team), and so on as you traverse the various levels of granularity. More to come on this later as we explore exactly how to identify and assign specific characteristics to each quadrant at each holonic level in the organization. The goal is to be able to produce a comprehensive and cohesive set of information that will be used to capture both the 'as-is' state as well as the 'to-be' future image that the Modernization or Transformation effort seeks to create. The difference between those two views will be used to identify a set of change initiatives that constitute a straw man proposal that can in turn be used to drive out a more comprehensive approach for the program.

For programs that have been successful, they've had to address all four of this model's aspects at one time or another, whether they were explicitly included in the original plan or not. They are inherently part of the problem to be solved. You can't do only one, two, or even three quarters of a puzzle and call it done. You have to complete all four quarters to accomplish the goal. The commonality that puzzles have with the concept of holons is that individual pieces will cross over boundaries and interlock with each other to create a strong and unified whole. The result is an image of something that is, from up close, obviously made up of many small pieces, but when you step back it presents itself as a single clear vision. Each piece is not only *integrated* with the others in a coordinated fashion to compose the whole, but each is also *integral* in that it is not omittable or removable without eliminating the wholeness of the final product. Given this idea of every piece being an absolutely necessary component within a complete and comprehensive overall approach, going forward, this four-quadrant visualization method will be referred to as the Integral Modernization and Transformation model (IMT).

To summarize, each of the four quadrants has their own characteristics and components, while collectively they describe the overall state of an organizational holon. When looking at each quadrant individually for any given holon, one aspect may be more or less developed and mature than another. The overall evolution and maturity of a holon is driven and defined by the interplay and relationships across all four aspects. Each piece to this puzzle has a unique shape unto itself, and when connected to the others creates a larger yet still unique result. The four aspects combine to make one, but that one is unlike any other. In order to better understand each unique scenario that may exist, and to be able to build our strategy around them as a whole, we need a clear definition of what constitutes 'maturity' that can be used for elaboration within the IMT model. That is the next piece needed to solve the puzzle of why most Modernization and Transformation initiatives are failing. The concept of maturity is important to introduce here because the main point of the overall initiative is to bring the company up to the next level and beyond. Therefore, what we need is a definition of relative maturity that is capable of being applied at the aspect/quadrant level, each sub-holon level, and ultimately to the organization as a whole.

Big Pieces - Stages of Maturity

It will always be true that every individual, team, environment, and organization will evolve and change over time. As time passes, each one of these four aspects progressively becomes more capable of fully integrating the lessons learned from prior experience while simultaneously moving forward to bigger and (usually) better things. Being cognizant of this evolutionary progress is crucial to understanding where an organization currently stands and where it needs to go. If a Modernization or Transformation strategy is to be successful, it will need to be based on a solid understanding of the current state of the organization across all four IMT quadrants. Therefore, a clear map must be provided that can be used to identify any 'you are here' points of reference that can be applied to each element of the company (Personal, Culture, Employment or Organizational). To be able to complete this initial orientation and determine where each of the four aspects currently stands on that ongoing journey, it helps to divide the larger evolutionary continuum into a manageable number of stages. Defining relative stages of maturity allows for highlighting common characteristics that exist at each stage. These characteristics can later be used to determine where something or someone stands on the overall path and what their next step is on their evolutionary journey.

Maturity and development models have been in use for many decades across a wide variety of contexts and practices. When considering the potential number and variety of developmental themes that occur across all four of the IMT quadrants, trying to accommodate all of the related studies and models that already exist might seem a bit overwhelming. There are several models describing individual human maturity that are based on psychology and human developmental stages. There are also social evolution models that trace our history through the development of family groups, tribes, empires, and nation states. More familiar to people in business and technology are maturity models that address process maturity, agile maturity, or how organizational 'consciousness' moves away from outdated and overly rigid structures toward a more free-flowing, self-organizing and self-managing "Teal" level [12]. Many of these models leverage a common practice of rainbow color-coded stages to portray a progression along a continuum. Even subtle human energy systems, like chakras, are frequently used as a parallel to define physical, psychological, and spiritual development through a series of rainbow-colored energy points. What may seem like a broad range of diverse and incongruous topics actually have significant commonalities that we can effectively use within the IMT model.

For purposes of creating an IMT map that can be used to identify the current or future state of an entity, the common contents of these existing models can be encapsulated into seven major stages of maturity. These stages can be applied to any one of the IMT quadrants individually and can also be applied to a person, team, process, technology, policy, or the organization as a whole. The seven stages are consolidations of what many other maturity models have used to differentiate between levels, so much of what is described below may already be familiar in some form or fashion, but it provides a single definition of relative maturity that is needed to move to the next step in the development of the IMT model.

Before we proceed, there is a critical element of this maturity model that needs to be understood when discussing the various stages. The thing to note is that what is defined as more 'mature' is not necessarily 'better' than any of the prior stages. This is because each stage that is being described both includes and transcends the previous stages, meaning that when moving to a higher order stage there is a capability of naturally handling more breadth, diversity, and complexity than there was in prior stages. The prior stages are progressively incorporated, not left behind, as depicted in the image below:

Each stage has its own inherent limitations that are not apparent to those operating within that stage at the time, but once they get beyond that stage, they are able to overcome and integrate the characteristics of prior stages in a more effective manner.

This allows for the pursuit and achievement of new levels of significance and complexity that are now available to them at the next stage. Therefore, it is perhaps better to think of these stages as cumulative rather than mutually exclusive. For the IMT model, the stages of maturity are:

- Surviving
- Connected
- Confident
- Purposeful
- Transparent
- Intuitive
- Transcendent

Because growth and maturity to a higher order stage transcends but includes all prior stages, there remain elements of these stages in all people and organizations. Although some of the characteristics and behaviors detailed below may be periodically observed, subsequent stages must also be considered to determine if specific circumstances are triggering lower stage behaviors because the moment and context calls for it, or if there are true limitations that are preventing the progress to higher levels of maturity. That said, let's start with the description of the most basic level of maturity that speaks directly to our innate 'adapt or die' evolutionary drive – the basic need for survival.

Surviving

The Surviving stage is the foundational beginnings of the IMT maturity model upon which all other stages are built. This is the "Me" phase where individuals, teams, and organizations are characterized as having a predominate focus on their own self-preservation and personal wellbeing. This level represents a fight to scratch out some modicum of continued existence, a fight that inherently carries with it an attitude of prioritizing one's own concerns over everything else at all times. While this may be most evident in how people behave relative to each other, it is also reflected in organizations that put themselves above all others, often putting moral principles and legalities to the side for their own needs. These types of behaviors are driven by an underlying belief that to ensure continued survival, one's own security and safety must be protected at all costs and by any means possible.

Embedded within this self-protective belief structure is an innate view that the outside world is a hostile environment. This creates a feeling that there is an ongoing power struggle between oneself and everything else 'out there'. Trying to survive under such perilous circumstances results in people making simplistic black-and-white distinctions to deal with a world that they perceive as being full of danger and sinister competitive forces. The common understanding at this stage is that safety can only be achieved by showing superior strength and defeating one's foes. Therefore, they act as if there is only the strong and the weak, 'my' way or 'your' way, and absolutely nothing in between.

By being centered in this worldview of 'the strong versus the weak', companies operating at the Surviving stage may unwittingly provide an open door to selfish individuals who believe they can be successful by directly imposing their will on others. Companies at this level naturally attract these types of opportunists who think and act with a combative, warrior-like attitude where 'might makes right' and gaining more power is a reward unto itself. These types of cunning, and often unprincipled, people believe that exerting raw personal power is the way to address a supposed world of scarcity as well as any perceived threats to their own well-being. Projecting power and displays of fearsomeness, they will pick fights, break rules, and get into trouble with very little awareness or concern for the consequences. These people cannot be reasoned with because they project all of their problems as being caused by the world 'out there'. This projection can directly transfer into being one of the foremost characteristics in the overall company culture. An organization can exhibit these same types of behaviors in how it approaches competition or how it justifies aggressive opposition to oversight or regulation. In a situation where asserting its power is ineffective, a sense of victimhood may immediately take over. When it does, there is never an admission of fault or of being wrong when operating at this level.

While at this stage, continuous attempts to demonstrate power and dominance over others is the primary relationship dynamic that exists across all organizational levels. For such companies, this dynamic often becomes much more visible and overt the higher you go up the leadership chain. Power at this stage is exercised through the use of aggression, fear, force, and intimidation to gain the upper hand. The underlying (and perhaps subconscious) belief at work is that order can be maintained, and overall stability achieved, through establishing one's own power ranking relative to the personal power of others. This level of maturity is the equivalent of the primitive and animalistic concept of the Alpha Male that can be seen in gorillas, lion prides, and wolf packs. Each individual's needs are either met by making demands of those that are deemed weaker, or abjectly submitting to those that are stronger in order to be protected and taken care of. Knowing one's relative rank determines how to treat the person on the other side of the table in any given encounter. This power dynamic is not necessarily limited to intra-office relationships, as younger or smaller organizations often end up submitting to the coercive will of one or two key customers or clients that provide the lion's share of revenues and are deemed to be the source of the company's going concern. In those cases, it is as if the company does not 'outrank' the customer and must bend over backwards to meet its demands.

The predominate drive for self-preservation and well-being that exists at this stage is what determines what each individual or organization perceives to be their core needs. These needs are typically oriented around material security in having at least a minimum level of revenue or income continuing to come in. This is often the only true concern. This minimalistic definition of 'needs' that is seen at the Surviving level reflects an egocentric viewpoint that is completely focused on achieving personal and individual safety. Many maturity models of human development state that people operating at a level of simple survival find their own sense of safety through meeting the most basic human survival needs such as having adequate food and shelter. In a business context, both for companies and employees, this translates to a singular focus on financial stability. The main goal is to continue to get paid but the pursuit of that goal is consistently felt to be under threat because there is also an ongoing sense of fear and unpredictability that it might end at any moment. The challenge that arises when being completely driven by such a simple survival instinct is that resulting actions are predictably impulsive, chaotic, and exhibit an overall lack of self-control.

Company processes and budgeting strategies at this stage will reflect a similar type of chaotic and ad-hoc nature. When operating at the Surviving level an organization tends to only be able to focus on one aspect of a situation at one time and is rarely able to focus on that one thing for an extended period of time. The orientation is completely around the present moment which in turn makes the environment highly reactive and volatile. There is no true capability for long-term planning as the impulsivity that exists will result in constantly changing priorities driven by perceived opportunities that must be immediately taken advantage of. This is where decision making is often driven by the HiPPO effect, where the 'highest paid person's opinion' determines how the group will proceed and everyone else defers or panders to that person's statements and position. For each decision point that arises, the short-term focus is directly tied to some perceived need for immediate gratification and the HiPPO, playing the Alpha role, barks out the commands that everyone else will follow instantaneously and without question.

The technology and skills that exist at the Surviving level are equally short-sighted and driven by the need for immediate action. The technology and tools to be used for various initiatives will be those that are readily available and most likely free or very low cost. This often leads to large gaps in what many would consider minimum standard capabilities, protections, and implementations across the company, creating a significant increase in risk to the business. Therefore, at the Surviving stage there is virtually no concept of an Enterprise Architecture. The piecemeal approach is heavily driven by the chaotic and impulsive nature that exists throughout the rest of the organization. There is a general lack of cohesion between business operations and technology infrastructure. In terms of skill sets, segregation and isolation of individual specializations are the norm, often creating single points of failure for the organization overall. There commonly exists a clear division of labor that differentiates the 'chiefs' from the 'foot soldiers', and also creates a separation of skill sets that exist with each group of workers. Due to the chaotic nature of the organization, the lack of long-term planning and the ad-hoc approach to technology, individual heroism is generally cultivated, encouraged, and rewarded accordingly.

Overall rewards and recognition are similarly driven by the primitive wolf-pack mentality of 'might makes right'. The Surviving level of maturity operates on the premise that every interaction is in effect some form of competition. Arising from that competitive nature is an unbridled drive to dominate and conquer rivals, where perceived rivals could be anyone, including internal colleagues, business partners or external competitors. The relationship of domination and submission defines how basic 'survival' needs are met, as those that exert their dominance over others receive more attention, recognition, rewards, and promotions. Those who have risen to leadership positions by exerting their personal power tend to command and demand attention from those within the company as well as from others outside the organization in an attempt to continually establish their dominance. The additional trait that this stage breeds is a general disregard for the feelings of others. There is a working assumption that people see, hear, and feel exactly the same as everyone else and therefore strength is the only differentiator to be recognized. This contributes to an environment of 'every man for himself' where loyalty and allegiance are bought by sharing the spoils of victory with those who could not take it for themselves.

Although still evident in many individuals and groups, it is rare for Surviving to be the overall stage of maturity for a business today. There are examples of where this level is still seen and, in some cases even appropriate. This stage of maturity can be highly suitable for truly hostile environments, such as prisons, combat zones, and openly violent inner cities. Street gangs and mafias instinctively operate at this level. In each of these cases the sought-after stability is achieved mostly through fear, loyalty, and 'family' where there is not any scalable hierarchy or job titles. Members do what they are told with no questions asked if they want to continue being protected and rewarded by those in power. These types of organizations are inherently fragile because leaders regularly resort to public displays of cruelty and punishment, using the resulting fear and submission to keep the organization together and the troops in line. Working at the Surviving stage rarely creates an environment that breeds long term loyalty and engagement because there is no true connection between any two individuals or entities.

Connected

The second stage of IMT maturity is characterized by a solid sense of connection and bonding with others. To be more specific, the bonds being forged here are with *some* others but not *all* others. Having grown beyond the self-centered traits of the Surviving stage, stronger human connections have now taken hold through the emergence of teams or groups that act like family units. These small close-knit teams reflect a movement from egocentric to ethnocentric behaviors where what was once 'every man for himself' at the Surviving stage has now become an attitude of 'us versus them' in the Connected stage. There is strong cooperation that occurs with the members of one's own team or group, but very little cooperation happens with others because those that are deemed 'different' or 'other' are viewed with distaste and suspicion. If the 'others' are to be interacted with at all, the belief is that they must be effectively controlled in a way that provides 'us' with what we want and need. This relationship dynamic is the genesis of the chasm between 'the business' and IT where heavy controls and demands are placed on technology delivery teams to 'hold them accountable' and 'meet their commitments'. The previous internal group dynamic of 'might makes right' at the Surviving stage has now evolved to become an outward dynamic where the will of the group is imposed on anyone considered to be an 'outsider', and oftentimes the technology 'geeks' are effectively treated as outsiders in comparison to those operating the rest of the business.

The value system that exists at the Connected level is based on a desire for stability that seeks to be organized around a single accepted definition of what is 'right'. This causes much of the thinking to be absolutistic and bureaucratic, where the belief is that the group's way of doing things is defensibly the one and only 'right' way and that the authority overseeing and protecting that 'right' way is enshrined in a rigid hierarchy. Therefore, acceptance is only given to those who unfailingly observe group norms, and preference is granted to those that are capable of showing respect to the hierarchy by being appropriately diplomatic. This is the stage of long-standing bureaucracies commonly seen in governmental organizations, organized religions, and the military establishment where one's role and rank directly defines the level and breadth of authority.

Well defined structures and roles are a major feature of organizations and teams operating at the Connected stage. For the individuals there is a desired sense of belonging that is met through being able to assume one's place in both a team and within the hierarchy. The feeling of 'safety in numbers' that is sought at this stage is reflected in the creation and perpetuation of a more stable and scalable organization. This individual need for belonging also results in people actively and deliberately striving for approval and acceptance. Group norms become internalized and lead to a type of thinking that is dominated by whether one has the right appearance, behavior, and thoughts to fit in. There is a related influence on the overall environment in that expectations and demands of conformity by every member of the company become overt and commonplace. The workplace itself carries a mandate of convention, conformity, and socially expected behavior that must be met in order to gain approval.

The drive for conformity paired with the absolutistic attitude of 'there is only *one* right way' also manifests as an environment of rigid compliance. The term 'command and control' is an accurate descriptor for those operating at the Connected stage due to the notion that leaders are assumed to be the originators and stewards of 'the right way', and they will direct the rest of the group on exactly how they are expected to act, execute, and conform. This often leads to a related underlying belief at this stage that deems workers to be inherently lazy and dishonest, and therefore a strong set of processes, roles, and rewards is intended to get an acceptable level of productive hours out of them. Regardless of the level of truth behind that assumption, the people across the hierarchy readily fall into their assigned roles and comply accordingly, consistently being put in a position to log extra hours to keep things 'on track'. This establishes the accepted system where everyone has an implicit understanding of the organizational norms and does their part to maintain the stability of the group.

While the Surviving stage was completely chaotic, impulsive and ad-hoc, the Connected stage brings about the overt use of processes, rules, laws, and regulations. Stability and order are enforced through the use of thoroughly documented procedures and rules. There is an expectation for each person to do their duty and show discipline through following all established processes to the letter. As a result, the use of rigid techniques such as the Responsibility Assignment Matrix (RACI) originates at this level. Detailed definitions of who does what for each and every task, milestone, and decision point are intended to remove any risk of confusion regarding roles and responsibilities.

Through the creation and continued development of such comprehensive processes, large amounts of business knowledge effectively become embedded in the organization itself. By way of these existing processes and their embedded knowledge, organizations and teams at the Connected stage now have the capability to plan for both the medium and long term. Again, driven by the desire for stability and the belief in the *one* right way enshrined in their extensive documentation, both the planning and the scalability of the organization reflect an assumption of minimal change over longer periods of time. Therefore, future planning at this stage is based completely on past experiences, where outcomes are predetermined before work begins, and the planning itself is completely separate from the subsequent execution of those plans. With all of these built-in assumptions and experiences that go into planning, when work begins, the push for order, compliance, and project predictability become recurring themes for leadership and project management.

In line with the drive for stability, the technology and skills at the Connected level are typically those that are well proven. Tried and true technologies are preferred even if they are much more costly, as stability and knowledge of past successes are of higher value than the perceived risks of anything new and relatively unknown. Given the proclivity for thorough documentation, Enterprise Architecture models such as the Zachman Framework and TOGAF (The Open Group Architecture Framework) originate and find extensive use at this stage, although they are most often used in an 'Ivory Tower' type of isolation separating the architects from the developers performing the actual implementations. Within the constraints of the given Enterprise Architecture, team member skill sets are leveraged and exhibited in a very disciplined manner, because wandering off from the established methods and approach is frowned upon. Minor best practices have become more commonplace to counteract the fragility inherent in the volatile nature of the Surviving stage, yet in practice the teams are still highly reactive and somewhat ad-hoc when it comes to responding to issues. There is an increased amount of firefighting that occurs at this level as production support activities are still explicitly separated from new development initiatives. Development work happens within a highly structured set of processes and frameworks and then those teams 'hand off' responsibility for the system to operational teams. These support teams have to deal with the realities of the unexpected and unforeseen while not having the same type of comprehensive processes and structures available to them to help respond more predictability.

Rewards and recognition at the Connected level are also very much in line with the attitudes of hierarchy and conformity that exist at this stage. Relative merit and ranking, typically directly tied to one's role and position, determine compensation and rewards. Since stability is paramount, innovation is not rewarded (and potentially discouraged outright) and any criticism or opposition to the established norms is viewed with suspicion and disdain. Those that speak up against any perceived wrongs or shortcomings are effectively silenced through the review, reward and recognition processes that favor those that conform and remain quiet. Those who do what is 'right' are rewarded, while those who do what is 'wrong' are punished, and potentially even rejected and jettisoned from the group or organization altogether. On the other hand, those individuals that are especially skilled at tactical diplomacy become the 'ladder-climbers' that move up the hierarchy of the organization while gaining higher levels of reward, recognition, and authority. Successes seen at the Connected stage will start to generate a broader sense of confidence across the organization.

Confident

The third stage of IMT maturity occurs when a clear and distinct sense of confidence emerges for both people and the companies they work for. This is the level of experts and achievers. This stage contains yet another progression of the power theme relative to what is seen at the Surviving and Connected stages, as power at this level is now a form of willpower that can be more effectively controlled and directed. This newfound capability of self-control results in a non-dominating type of power that was not possible in the more impulsive and instinctive prior stages, where at first, domination drove submission, and then conformity. There is a certain energy and effectiveness that comes with the exertion of controlled will power that results in an orientation of operational efficiency, increased profits, and broader wealth generation. This is the stage that most large organizations operate from today. It is the stage of achievement, where the belief is: If I am faster, smarter, and more innovative than others in understanding and manipulating the world, then I will achieve more success, wealth, market share, or whatever else I desire. For those with this achievement mindset, more is generally considered better. This stage is characterized by a general attitude of 'Profit over People' in that management's thinking is centered on shareholder value, competition, innovation, and financial performance. When describing anything that can be leveraged by the company for profitable pursuits, the label of 'resources' is applied to people as well as financial and technology assets. Behind this profit-oriented form of management thinking is a subtle shift from 'command and control' behaviors to a 'predict and control' approach that seeks to mitigate any perceived risks to financial and delivery targets which have predetermined timelines and milestones.

Even though this stage is still similar to the Surviving and Connected stages in being solidly materialistic, there is now a new capacity and acceptance for people to question authority, group norms, and the status quo. The difference from the strict conformity enforced in the prior stage to preserve 'the one right way' is that now questioning the current state is viewed as a means through which improvements can be made that ultimately will lead to increased profits, although the rate of actual change can still be remarkably slow. The type of questioning that happens at this level is itself directed at tangible, material things such as business cases, processes, tools, policies, and organizational structures. The ongoing metaphor at this level is that the business operates like a machine that can be scientifically studied, analyzed, automated, and optimized, which results in an abundance of manufacturing analogies being used throughout companies that are not in the business of actual manufacturing. The pervasiveness of scientific thinking and the associated empiricism, where only that which can be seen and touched is worth consideration, also has a counter-belief at this stage. Anything that sounds 'hippie' or 'touchy-feely', such as anything that speaks to internal aspects of feelings, empathy, spirituality, or transcendence, is typically brushed aside as being less valuable and not important. Those operating at the Confident stage as 'experts' are not yet equipped to address the difficulty in believing or working with anything that cannot empirically be proven or observed. With this being the most prevalent stage of maturity in business today, these experts are commonly known to spend inordinate amounts of time on exterior realities as the way by which they expect to accomplish their goals, through things such as water-tight analysis of data, quantified argumentation, and extensive modeling of systems and operations. This penchant for scientific knowledge and expertise creates a bias against collaboration and deep, empathic listening because Emotional Intelligence (EQ) is typically valued less at this level. Experts at this level are apt to perceive and believe that their way is the 'right' way to do things and will readily dismiss other points of view. With the discounting of matters regarding emotions and general well-being, any discussion around social responsibility for the organization at large is deemed a distracting obligation at this stage because the belief is that such activities do not directly drive increased profitability and shareholder value.

Processes and budgeting functions are also reflective of profit-orientation at this stage. Operating with a shareholder perspective, everything is oriented around maximizing profit through increasing revenues and optimizing the efficiency of operations, i.e., lowering costs. There is a project orientation to all work efforts that is often paired with heavy annual budgeting processes, cost accounting practices, elaborate controls around expenditure requests and approvals, and a significant amount of estimating activity and business case development embedded within those control processes. For those presenting new project proposals this requires a strong capability to analyze data and to make quantified arguments to garner support for the initiatives and requested funding, although oftentimes these initial arguments are not referenced again nor compared against actual results once funding has been obtained. At this stage, these types of functions and approaches across the organization also produce a glorification of decisiveness because strategy and its timely execution are primary concerns for everyone involved, especially the shareholders. Everything comes with a sense of urgency and an understanding that there is no time to waste, especially for those trying to meet quarterly numbers and targets. In direct support of these attitudes, the main metrics tracked and reported out are around projects being 'on-time' and 'under-budget', where RAG reports (Red, Amber/Yellow, Green) have high frequency usage and visibility. Most mid-project adjustments are made to 'get back to green' while retaining the original parameters set around the effort's cost, time, and scope estimations and commitments.

At this stage, individuals, teams and companies will sometimes run initiatives to implement new ways of working, such as Lean, Agile, and DevOps, but it is usually driven out of a competitive or 'me too' nature that sees other, more mature organizations being successful in those areas and with those techniques. The underlying behavior is still mostly driven by the project management 'iron triangle' of cost, time, and scope, where delivering on 'commitments' is still paramount. This further reinforces the divide between 'Business' and 'IT'. This environmental paradox typically results in mandated and dogmatic approaches to new ways of working that end up causing more problems than they solve, both in business value derived and employee morale. Terminology and actions will be learned and practiced by people to show that they are acting as expected, but underlying changes in mindset and behavior do not necessarily occur which would actually unleash the intended benefits. Those individuals who have obtained formal certifications are deemed to be the 'experts' and, frequently, these 'experts' have not had practical experience with other, more mature organizations. Consequently, these individuals will oversee the usage of these methods with a dogmatic attitude of enforcing strict process compliance such as was seen in the Connected stage. A term such as "Agile in Name Only" (AINO) is a good example of what accurately describes the phenomenon seen at this stage where superficial changes mask a deeper resistance to change as well as a general level of frustration that exists under the surface.

The Confident stage is the stage that glorifies expertise and knowledge. Expertise can be directly leveraged for profit, so being an expert or leader in a field brings with it a certain level of distinction. Various types of expertise are normally segregated within the organization, which can clearly be seen in the absolute distinction between 'the Business' and 'IT'. This opposition of seemingly disparate types of expertise brings with it a continuation of the 'us versus them' theme from the Connected stage. Business experts often perceive IT to be slow, expensive, and not in tune with the business, while IT people perceive their business counterparts to be technically inept and not capable of knowing or communicating exactly what it is that they want. They each have their own types of expertise that may ultimately come together to provide viable solutions, but the day-to-day behavior is still heavily influenced by the 'us versus them' mentality retained from the Connected stage when IT is treated as a service provider to the rest of the business. This 'order maker, order taker' model remains prevalent in Confident companies because the work performed is driven by the estimations and negotiations that occur when building the up-front business case and project requirements which become the 'commitments' on which IT teams must provide 'on time' and 'under budget' delivery.

Due to the business demands regarding profitability and cost control, IT leadership will frequently look to emerging technologies as a combination of newer, more capable, more stable, and less expensive solutions that will provide the desired operational savings and predictability. Yet senior leadership at this level may only give serious consideration to those solutions that have some sort of proven track record so as not to be deemed overly risky. For technology departments at this stage, many are making their first forays into open-source and cloud technologies but only with providers that have established histories of usage and stability, and often with the company taking a very timid 'dip your toe in the water' type of approach. Enterprise Architecture groups are beginning to come down from their 'Ivory Tower'; becoming more engaged with actual implementations through the use of Solution and Technical Architect positions. The desire for both cost effectiveness and predictability at this stage also leads to more automation of maintenance tasks, proactive IT support procedures, standardization in responding to issues, formal asset management, and a drive to analyze and optimize all systems and processes.

In larger, well established 'cash cow' companies, the chasm between business and IT is often noticeably wider when looking at how they identify new initiatives. Architecture and technology experts frequently begin working with emerging technology platforms independent of current business drivers and strategies under the guise of 'future business needs and benefits', perhaps calling them 'proof of concept' efforts to address the perceived risk of the unknown while still being allowed to explore and learn new technical skill sets. At the same time those on the business side desire to make significant leaps forward in product and service offerings in the name of increased revenue opportunities, and yet they may not have a good grasp on what it takes to enable these new capabilities digitally or drive incremental and evolutionary change with a customer-centric approach. This disconnect between business strategy and the 'as-is' and 'to-be' enterprise architecture is particularly noticeable in these types of environments. Bringing forward ideas and proposals through the lens of their own areas of expertise, each side speaks in their own language which the other side cannot understand or identify with. This severely limits the opportunities for collaboration and consensus. In both cases, funding proposals and approvals are based on an expected return on investment (ROI) that always seems to be a 'no-brainer' decision based on the numbers provided. To get the proposed numbers to surpass this 'no-brainer' threshold, each effort turns into an outsized initiative that ends up further alienating the two sides. Both groups are driven by the current environment to ask for large amounts of funding to justify work around large initiatives that include extensive scope (often called 'feature bloat' or 'gold plating') so they can claim their share of the annual funding available and also avoid the possibility of having to return to the well for funding again and again in the future. Such super-sized initiatives come with grand expectations of massive gains in revenues and/or cost controls that will supposedly drive significant increases in company profitability and shareholder value. More often than not, these types of initiatives fail to produce the expected returns, while keeping the organization relatively stagnant in their current offerings and capabilities (hence the periodic need for massive and disruptive Modernization and Transformation programs!). As projects and spending progress throughout the year, formal budgetary shifts often happen in later months of the year that redirect funds from the 'haves' to the 'have-nots'. This frequently creates an environmental and cultural belief system of 'use it or lose it' that results in a dilution of efforts on lower value activities. This also leads to a cultural characteristic of senior leaders identifying with their budgets and headcount as the outward signs of their relative level of personal power, importance, distinction, and authority, all of which are very much reflective of the 'achiever' mentality prevalent at this stage of maturity.

Reward programs at this level reflect a mindset of achieving profitable and timely results in the prescribed fashion. Given the plan-driven project orientation that exists at the Confident stage, individuals that perform heroic efforts to keep a project on time and under budget will be recognized and rewarded accordingly. In line with the dominant theme of shareholder profits, compensation structures at this level commonly expand to include things like profit sharing, stock plans, and other incentives designed to keep the focus on maximizing profitability and EBITDA (Earnings Before Interest Taxes Depreciation and Amortization). The orientation of most incentives, rewards, and recognition at this stage is around motivating individuals in ways that drive positive financial outcomes for the business. For the Confident organization, a meritocracy emerges that encourages the use of expertise for innovation and improvement, as well as being accountable for delivering in a timely and cost-effective manner.

Many companies currently operate at the Confident stage, building brands, products and services that outwardly convey their expertise, certainty and "proven best way" to achieve their goals in a complex world. This stage brings with it a high risk of promoting unethical behavior if adequate checks and balances are not in place. For example, the value system of Wall Street with its premium on publicly held companies achieving quarterly targets at all costs (i.e., 'Profit over People') can result in a toxic mix of greed and apparent certainty that incentivizes fraudulent and unethical activities that have been seen in many of the recent financial institution scandals and full-blown social disasters such as the Collateralized Debt Obligations (CDO) market crash that led to the Great Recession in 2008. Bad things happen when the profit motive becomes more powerful than an organization's purpose and reason for being.

Purposeful

The Purposeful stage flips the 'Profit over People' mindset of the Confident stage upside down and becomes much more about 'People over Profit' as organizational strategy and execution are superseded by company culture as paramount. Going beyond the prior stages where the focus was on individual, internal, and material successes, this level now values relationships over outcomes which inherently includes a newfound concern and sensitivity for people's feelings and wellbeing. This shift is shown through the daily interactions between colleagues as well as a better overall relationship and understanding of the company's customers. The belief system espoused at this level is that if attention is consciously directed toward helping people (both employees and customers) and cultivating a sense of empathy and understanding, then profits will follow accordingly.

Through the first four stages of maturity, this is the first level at which we start to see specific attention being placed on the interior aspects represented by the left side of the IMT four quadrant model (Personal and Cultural). The emergence of true consideration for how people think and feel results in behaviors that show more compassion, altruism, and broader integration across the organization. There is value placed in community, harmony, tolerance, and equality with a focus on empowerment. This is the time at which the company culture consistently demonstrates the belief that all perspectives are valued, deserve respect, are to be heard and considered in open dialog, and that the best solutions and innovations can come from any person at any level. This translates to a leadership focus that goes beyond the shareholders of the Confident stage to now include management, employees, customers, suppliers, local communities, society at large, and the environment. The role of leadership is to make the right trade-offs so all stakeholders can thrive. Social responsibility has become integral to how a Purposeful company does business as opposed to the Confident stage where it was viewed as a distracting obligation. Leaders maintain that while the multiple stakeholder perspective may sometimes mean higher costs in the short term, taking this view will deliver benefits for everyone in the long run including shareholders. It is because of this impetus toward general wellbeing that companies begin to sense that people are no longer robotically going through the motions and that true transformation is beginning to take place. Motivation and engagement are elevated, the workplace is more energetic and dynamic, and genuine business agility and adaptability are within reach.

For Purposeful companies, the guiding metaphor has shifted from viewing the 'organization as a machine' to one of the 'organization as a family' that understands the inherent benefits of cohesion and flexibility that come from a foundation of strong ties and relationships. This attitude and value system permeates leadership communications at this level, reinforcing the idea that all employees, regardless of position, are part of the same family. They are in it together, always ready to help each other out, and are genuinely concerned about being there for one another. An interesting dynamic at this stage is that, given the family orientation, there is a mindset of relativism that allows for a broader understanding and acceptance of those individuals who may be operating at prior stages of maturity and yet this does not inhibit the integration of those individuals into the overall company culture. Research estimates that only about 10% of the adult population truly operates at this level of maturity, but this level 'animates downward an ethos' that is readily received by the diplomats, experts and achievers that are seen in the Connected and Confident stages[13]. The values of community, group process and emotional sanctity that emanate from this stage become aspirational values that are adopted by these people who in turn become significant contributors and participants for related company initiatives and activities. It is at this stage where leadership begins to realize that the organization is a complex adaptive system that needs to be influenced and interacted with appropriately to realize benefits rather than trying to exert some form of control over the environment itself.

The Purposeful stage also has strikingly different characteristics around the needs and identity of the people, as the desire for autonomy, growth, and freedom are being paired with a positive acceptance of accountability and responsibility. As organizations move into this phase there is a groundswell in demands for broader empowerment, increased levels of motivation and a push to create great workplaces. Collaboration and consensus are much more prevalent at this level compared to the belief in and deference to the 'select few' that was seen in prior stages, even though for large groups and organizations gaining consensus can be inherently difficult. That said, breakthroughs at the Purposeful stage are evidenced by companies that have been able to create a new organizational model through employee empowerment, a multiple stakeholder perspective, and establishing a values-driven culture with inspirational purpose. Some well-known examples are Starbucks, Southwest Airlines, Ben & Jerry's, and The Container Store [14] .

Empowerment at this stage retains the merit-based hierarchy seen in prior stages but begins to push as many decisions as possible down to frontline workers, allowing them to make decisions without managerial approval. Those on the frontline are trusted to make better decisions because they are in touch with the many, smaller day-to-day problems and therefore can devise better solutions. People are empowered to seek creative solutions to problems wherein employees at prior stages were required to follow the rules and to seek formal approval for any potential deviation. Therefore, the Purposeful stage sees a significant increase in the rate and impact of innovations and market disruptors.

There is a significant challenge that arises while companies traverse this stage because decentralization and empowerment on a large scale is not easy. Managers that were previously the authority figures and taskmasters are effectively asked to share power and control. For many this is a very difficult transition, and many cannot make the shift without proactive help, coaching, and guidance from their executives and colleagues. Companies at the Purposeful stage invest time and effort in this space to clearly spell out what kind of leadership they expect from senior and middle managers. This managerial transition happens in the name of servant leadership where everyone in the company is expected to listen to subordinates, empower them, motivate them, and develop them. This can feel threatening to those that who have long believed that their responsibility as a manager is to tell employees exactly what to do with their time, often managing 'resource' allocations across multiple projects via spreadsheet, but now they are supposed to become a 'people person' and help their people grow. Their familiar ground is being taken out from under them and it can seem as if the company is becoming less and less stable. For the Purposeful organization, countering this uncertainty with a strong shared culture becomes the glue that keeps an organization from falling apart because employees are now being trusted to make decisions guided by shared values rather than by a thick book of policies and procedures.

Given the newfound attitude of 'people first', a Purposeful organization will begin to establish coordinated efforts around pursuing and realizing true diversity, inclusion and belonging across the company. These initiatives reflect a level of social awareness rooted in a value system that seeks to always do what is fair, right, and just for all humans, regardless of race, sex, or creed. With that same attitude of helping others, an increased level of servant leadership begins to take hold across the entire organization. Senior leaders are expected to be in service of those they lead and to personify the new values by being noble, generous, and empathetic. In light of continuing inequality and discrimination in the world at large, company executives can shepherd their organizations into the Purposeful stage by sharing their belief that there is more to life than the self-centered pursuit of career and financial success.

In the areas of processes and budgets, the focus at this stage reflects the expanded viewpoint that goes beyond shareholder concerns to include a much broader set of stakeholders. This means employees, customers, and other social concerns are seen to carry as much importance as profitability. The increase in collaboration at all levels creates an environment where groups with opposing views can work together and come to consensus. This in turn allows for the development of bottom-up processes, which is clearly different from the top-down decision making and directive nature that was seen in prior stages. More voices are being heard and are shaping the various ways of working into something much more team and group-oriented than a standardized and rigid sequencing of individual contributors with disparate skill sets. New organizational models and budgetary approaches will reflect the new attitudes of empowerment and orientation around shared values and purpose as the associated sense of trust equates to decision making being pushed down throughout the organization. Funding at this stage frequently shifts from projects to products or long-lived teams to help facilitate distributed decision making, but this comes with associated difficulties in determining how to address previous approaches and demands for estimation and realization of asset values used for capitalization and depreciation. The relationship to rules, processes and policies becomes more ambiguous at this stage because people are more adept at identifying the shortcomings inherent in prior stages, but they are not yet entirely effective in defining new alternatives.

The Purposeful stage brings multiple skill sets together around shared purpose, as dedicated cross-functional teams become the norm. Cooperation and partnership between business and IT people starts to emerge at this stage, beginning to build a bridge over the chasm that existed between the two sides in prior levels. Individual skills sets are no longer separated and isolated, as the concept of "T-shaped" skills allows people to have more diverse skill sets while still being able to have deep expertise in specific areas. As long as a team has the collective skills required to do the job, they are given the autonomy to complete deliverables in the best way they see fit. Team ownership at this stage supplants the issues that often arise in prior levels where an individual contributor would avoid responsibility and accountability simply by saying 'that's not my job'. This shift in ownership and accountability also leads to the broad use of 'swarming' where all team members with their complementary skills come together to help move along an effort that has gotten 'stuck' or is at risk of not being completed in a timely fashion.

Enterprise Architecture (EA) functions are more fully integrated at this phase as well, as technical expertise becomes embedded in the composition of a delivery team as opposed to having a clear distinction between Architects and Tech Leads. This results in more relativism being seen in the Enterprise Architecture domain, as componentized structures consisting of many specialized best fit solutions become more prominent. Whereas specific standards and constraints were the products of EA in prior stages, the Purposeful stage puts EA in a much more collaborative role where they provide guidance and insight to both technology and business colleagues during planning and implementation. The rapid evolution of technologies and available solutions is also often seen in multiple technologies being used to create and support multiple products and customer channels as opposed to pursuing outdated approaches that minimized and reduced the number of platforms and skills required in the organization. Beyond the application technologies, an expansion of data and analytics skills also begins tying together multiple aspects of the business in near-real time to facilitate better internal decision making as well as creating unified cross-platform and cross-channel customer experiences. At the Purposeful stage, the Enterprise Architecture is becoming less monolithic and more capable of enabling the increasing need for business and technical agility.

Rewards and recognition at this level reflect the company-wide values and support for employee wellbeing and engagement. The primary use of social recognition and intrinsic motivation that emerges at this stage is directly tied to an organizational belief that the best way to achieve strategic objectives is to cultivate positive behaviors based on company values and purpose, not simply meeting profit or other financial objectives. Financial considerations, both at the company and the individual level, begin to take a secondary position in order of importance. Employee motivation and engagement ascends to never before seen levels as companies recognize the benefits of paying staff enough to 'take the issue of money off of the table' while creating the environment needed for them to be successful. Employee motivation and engagement increases significantly in an environment where people can focus on pursuing a meaningful purpose with sufficient autonomy to get the job done and which also provides them with the ability to grow and master their chosen skills and areas of expertise[15]. This creates a virtuous cycle where business value and employee satisfaction become components of an ongoing feedback cycle that drives increasing benefits for everyone involved.

When leadership genuinely organizes around shared values it creates a vibrant culture where employees feel empowered and appreciated. The results for those that have made it to the Purposeful stage have had spectacular results and supporting research shows that values-driven organizations can outperform their peers by wide margins[16]. These companies put inspirational purpose and company culture at the heart of what they do. CEOs of Purposeful companies claim that promoting culture and shared values is their primary task. Human Resources and People Operations are elevated to a central role in these organizations, where a CHRO (Chief Human Resources Officer) or CPO (Chief People Officer) can be an influential member of the senior leadership team and a direct counselor and advisor to the CEO. Purposeful companies make large investments in training, culture initiatives, 360-degree feedback, succession planning and morale surveys. They are values-driven organizations, and their values are also on display for the public at large. For example, Southwest Airlines says they are in the business of 'freedom' because they are helping customers go where they normally wouldn't be able to go without their low fares. Ben & Jerry's believes they are not simply an ice cream company because they operate around a value system that shows care and stewardship for the earth and the environment. These companies are breaking down the barriers that used to exist between the purpose and operations of a for-profit company and the belief systems of the people that work for them. The result is a greater transparency of everything that goes into making great companies and great workplaces.

Transparent

The Transparent stage of maturity expands beyond Purposeful to include an innate drive to be completely open and honest in all communications and to operate with natural integrity and authenticity. For people and organizations at this stage everything is made available for review, analysis, and discussion while nothing is left 'behind the curtain'. Internal cohesion begins to take hold with integration and alignment occurring in every direction and across all pieces and parts that make up the whole. The Transparent stage represents this same ideal of wholeness that underpinned Carl Jung's concept of Individuation as well as the state of Self-Actualization in Maslow's well-known 'Hierarchy of Needs'. By attaining that state there is an undeniable drive to become the most that one can be. It is the difference between *knowing* your purpose and *living* your purpose. Honesty, creativity, integrity, authenticity, and meaning are the most highly regarded values at this level and are cultivated through communication, transparency, and truth. As a result, where the Purposeful stage brought diversity, inclusion, and belonging to the forefront, the Transparent stage brings a deeper, more concerted effort to root out any remnants of systemic and institutionalized discrimination in order to promote equality of opportunity over equality and homogeneity of outcomes. The Transparent organization strives to be a place where everyone is welcome and where they can be their unfiltered authentic selves.

Movement into the Transparent stage is considered to be more of a "monumental leap" forward than the slower evolutionary progression seen through the prior stages. This is because the whole paradigm by which people and organizations define themselves at this level changes from an ego-based approach to a completely universal one. Having managed to move above and beyond the prior stages to then discover the evolution of society reflected in their own existence, the realization is that it was absolutely necessary to pass through all the other stages to reach and be able to effectively manage the complexity of what is. For the first time, people and organizations are defined by accepting all other ways of being where they can see clearly now the value and purpose of all levels. At the Transparent stage there is a desire to transcend the lower levels while still including them, which is markedly different from the repression and exclusion of lower levels that happens in prior stages of maturity. This is an important characteristic to note because, as was noted within the concept of holons, each structure transcends but also includes the previous structures. At this stage, the aspects of the other stages are fully and consciously included, but up to this point evolving to a higher stage was usually done by repressing the so-called 'shadow material' that exists around the unsolved issues typical to lower stages. Tapping into the perspective of the Transparent stage, one can start a conscious process of reintegrating those shadows. This is the basis behind the internal cohesion that develops at this stage. Previously, the Confident stage judged those at the Surviving and Connected stages for placing crippling limitations on individual contributions outside of the imposed dogma, and the Purposeful stage judged those at the Confident stage for insensibility and callousness in the name of profits. The Transparent stage now realizes that each step was, and is, necessary for evolution and that this structure in itself is a step towards a more complex structure. Being at this stage comes with an understanding that evolution and change have always been happening and will continue to happen indefinitely. Therefore, an organization at this level defines its values accordingly and consciously aligns themselves in a way that will allow them to address future change and progress in an intentional and controlled manner. This is a distinctly different approach from prior stages where companies were in effect letting the odds decide when a need for change would appear and then reacting accordingly. Organizations at this stage are proactively fighting against the tendency to preserve the company culture in its current state so that it may continue to evolve and adapt in sync with an ever-changing and globalized world.

The Transparent organization understands that, for both companies and people, everything starts from the most basic structure and that the number of years does not necessarily determine the current stage or structure. It is determined by the degree of openness to change, the active working on improvement, the eagerness to take on new opportunities, and the wisdom gathered along the way. Progress is not made suddenly from one stage to the other, and not one person, team, or company is situated entirely in one particular stage. Rather, gradually, each one has different parts in different stages. The Transparent organization rejoices in having the opportunity to transcend shortcomings and engage everyone involved to actively develop towards the highest potential. Knowing that we exist in a world where everything changes, companies at this stage embrace the nature of the world instead of fighting against it. Being transparent includes having the courage to openly acknowledge and admit that nobody knows precisely what the future will bring.

In line with the idea of living one's purpose, this level is about finding a deeper meaning in work and in life, with the two frequently constituting two sides of the same coin. For many, that deeper meaning comes from being able to better understand one's own innate capabilities and gifts. Companies operating at the Transparent stage fully support employee individuality by creating an environment where everyone is able to bring the full expression of their authentic selves to work every day so that they may best apply their own unique strengths in support of the company's reason for being. For those who do not yet feel a particular sense of purpose, this can be a daunting task. For others who are gifted with a particular talent, their purpose may seem more obvious. Regardless of where each individual is on that journey of self-realization, the organization creates multiple opportunities for each person to play to their own unique strengths, focus on what they love to do, and pay attention to what is immediately in front of them. Whatever those things turn out to be, the expectation is only that they do it to the best of their ability. Employees are allowed to follow their joy, further develop their most obvious talents, and pursue their passion. This is somewhat counter-intuitive to prior stages, where individuals were expected to conform to generalized and comprehensive expectations of what every employee 'should' be and where their 'weaknesses' were explicitly called out as 'opportunities for development'. The advent of assessment techniques such as CliftonStrengths (formerly Clifton StrengthsFinder) highlights a shift toward playing to one's natural abilities and interests while moving away from each individual trying to be everything to everyone. Don Clifton's studies of human development made him realize that most of what we focus on is what is *wrong* with people as opposed to what is *right* about them. Psychologists in general describe this as a shift from a deficit to a strength-based paradigm that suggests that, as human beings, we are not problems waiting to be solved, but potential waiting to unfold. The Transparent organization is dedicated to recognizing what is right about each and every one of their people. Clifton himself wrote:

> *"There is no more effective way to empower people than to see each person in terms of his or her strengths."[17]*

Many people do not discover their purpose until quite late in life. However, when they look back, they realize that all the twists and turns had a reason and prepared them to give their own unique gifts in the most meaningful and fulfilling way. Operating at the Transparent stage creates an environment that harmonizes and integrates a shared journey of synchronicity that is constantly unfolding in front of everyone. Leadership at this stage is confident and rests assured that when employees commit their energy to their soul-purpose, all manner of unexpected events will occur to support them and the company overall.

Being open and honest about not knowing what the future holds, paired with a focus on passion and purpose may mean giving up a way of existence that once brought a sense of comfort, stability, and certainty. Working at the Transparent level may mean risking financial stability in the name of deeper meaning which can definitely be scary, but it is not something to be avoided. Organizations and people at this stage know that they will never be at ease with themselves and will not find internal stability if they do not follow their passion. The specter of spending the rest of your life feeling unfulfilled, depressed, or living with regrets is more than enough motivation to establish and pursue a living purpose.

Processes and financial concerns take on a very different flavor in the Transparent organization. Knowing there is not going to be any form of certainty and stability, light weight methods become the norm so that teams can focus on meaningful outcomes. The values and principles that form the foundation of Lean and Agile methods have become second nature at this stage, where there is value in accelerating learning, utilizing frequent feedback loops, and making 'pivot or persevere' decisions at each learning point. Optimizing the flow of work through the teams is accomplished by removing unnecessary overhead, controls and oversight as trust and transparency are fundamental to the autonomy and empowerment of the teams. Estimating work becomes virtually irrelevant knowing that the future is highly uncertain, so by trusting in the company's higher purpose the focus shifts to monitoring and assessing what 'is unfolding' versus what 'will be'. Teams have visibility into company finances and are trusted to make appropriate decisions regarding the time spent on pursuing projects and initiatives. Therefore, status reports and 'on time and under budget' discussions no longer exist. Incorporating the drive to be the best they can be, everyone in the organization fully embraces best practices with built-in quality methods and measures which are utilized unfailingly in every task they perform. All technology initiatives have highly strategic intent, are well coordinated and streamlined, and show valid business impacts. Technical, quality, and procedural capabilities become intertwined and inseparable, such as can be seen when automating a DevOps pipeline, utilizing telemetry data, blue/green deployments, A/B testing and other data-driven real time monitoring and feedback mechanisms.

In a similar vein, technologies and skill sets at this stage align with the concepts of purpose and transparency. The complete set of solutions provide a unified and transparent omnichannel customer experience. The underlying Enterprise Architectures that provide this customer experience consist of integrated and unified sets of fit-for-purpose solutions that are based on open communications between components via application program interfaces (APIs) and shared data. Having evolved out of Service Oriented Architectures (SOA), microservices architectures have become a common way of designing these types of software applications as suites of independently deployable services organized around business capabilities with automated deployment structures that provide intelligence in the endpoints and decentralized control of languages and data. Leveraging microservices and additional technologies such as virtual machines in cloud environments allows for these solutions to self-heal as needed based on system monitoring of performance and stability, as well as to automatically add or remove node instances to meet varying levels of customer usage and demand. Given the interconnectedness of these architectures, the skill sets required have also become more intertwined with team members who are required to be part developer, part tester, part architect, part infrastructure, and part operations all across a multitude of individual technologies and tools. Just as the human interactions across the organization represent a new level of complexity at this stage, microservices architectures reflect the same shift through technology in the way that components are connected, the way that they communicate, and how people collaborate to keep everything running.

Rewards and recognition at this stage are also very much about transparency and self-management with the goal being to create an immersive employee experience where people feel good and live with purpose. Having a deep connection and a sense of purpose at work results in increased energy and commitment. Employees bring their whole authentic selves to work and that self is recognized and valued by the organization. How the company does things drives and maintains the overall employee experience and transparency across the organization gives further insight into this value system. Companies at this stage begin to publish salaries (or at least salary ranges) to ensure that employees are being treated equitably and to remove any remnants of discriminatory decisions or pay gaps between various demographic groups. Periodic performance reviews are eliminated as people who understand the company's purpose begin to act with an entrepreneurial spirit and become a part of self-organizing teams. These teams take personal ownership and responsibility, reach their goals, and resolve tensions and conflicts in a constructive manner. What is rewarding to people at this stage is based on intrinsic motivation, peer feedback and meeting market and customer demands. People no longer receive pressure from the top, but they do want to know whether they are doing a good job. Therefore, self-managing teams measure things like team results and productivity and profit just like other organizations do at other stages. The difference in rewards and recognition at this stage is a focus on the team rather than individuals. Performance data is visible to everyone, which creates a culture of frequent feedback that generates both recognition and peer pressure to succeed. In place of managerial reviews, peer-based systems have become the norm in a more networked and integrated organization where feedback is seen as a form of reward.

For monetary compensation, organizations with self-managed teams may allow team members to look at the market to figure out the value of individual roles, determining if their salaries are in line with what others pay. After the initial value has been set, when someone is entitled to a raise because of good performance and/or reaching a higher experience level, colleagues may determine raises or individuals will 'self-set' their salary by either utilizing an established advice process or by making a pitch to a democratically chosen committee who will approve or deny the raise[18]. All of these methods are based on the organizational transparency of salaries, company finances, and the availability of funding for employee pay. As companies progress through this stage, identifying opportunities for various types of reward and recognition become more and more intuitive and instinctive for everyone involved.

Intuitive

The Intuitive stage is best characterized by the concept of a complex adaptive system (CAS). In the same sense that humankind has evolved through adaptation and ecological interactions with each other and the environment, Intuitive organizations mirror the complex nature of a human being in that they are made up of many diverse components intricately arranged into a unified whole while the overall entity's behavior and operation is constantly changing through continuous feedback and learning. This is the stage of true emergence where a company's purpose, people, processes, and technology are all capable of quickly becoming whatever their interactions with the world direct them to be. From a more academic perspective, the definition of a CAS is:

"A complex adaptive system is a system that is complex in that it is a dynamic network of interactions, but the behavior of the ensemble may not be predictable according to the behavior of the components. It is adaptive in that the individual and collective behavior mutate and self-organize corresponding to the change-initiating micro-event or collection of events. It is a "complex macroscopic collection" of relatively "similar and partially connected micro-structures" formed in order to adapt to the changing environment and increase their survivability as a macro-structure."[9]

Adapt or Die.

The story has come full circle with the confluence of human evolution and organizational evolution occurring at the Intuitive stage. Organizations at the Intuitive stage operate almost effortlessly without central control, even at a large scale, using systems based on peer-relationships that do not have a need for hierarchy or consensus. Unification and wholeness are reflected in the elimination of work personas, building on the prior stage where each person is now allowed to be their authentic self at all times. At the Intuitive stage, the organization is known to have a life and direction of its own. Instead of attempting to exert control or predict the future, members of the organization are invited to 'listen' to what the organization wants to become. The organization has a purpose of its own that is distinct from the purposes or objectives of its members, and it will continue to 'tell' those members what purpose it is meant to serve.

As a CAS, the organization consists of a number of elements (members or teams), which interact in non-linear ways to achieve the purpose of the system. These interactions between members are based on a few simple rules or guiding principles, and the nature of these relationships, and the substantial number of interactions between the elements results in emergent behavior. These organizational elements sense and gather information from both internal and external environments and react accordingly. Based on this gathered information, the elements self-organize by fluidly changing the relationships between themselves to adapt to the changes occurring in the environment. These organizational elements learn from experience and from the environment then adapt accordingly to ensure the survival of the company.

Companies at this stage have established true self-management across the whole organization which provides an innate capability for rapid change and adaptation driven by continuous interaction and experimentation with the outside world.

Learning is constant and continuously building a better understanding of what works and what doesn't, all the while allowing these 'micro-events' to reset plans and direction. Those operating at this level have an absolutely clear sense of independence and unity but understand that the nature of their true purpose is evolutionary and unpredictable. This gives them supreme confidence that they are attuned with what needs to be done and that what they are doing is making a difference in the world. Whether we are speaking about an individual, a team or an organization, what is clear at this stage is that it is nearly impossible to knock them off course with regards to their purpose-driven objectives. They are impervious to outside influences, especially from those still working through the challenges and deficiencies that exist in earlier stages. There is a continued drive to be fully integrated and cohesive internally, as was seen in the Transparent stage, but this now expands to a more outward facing worldview that seeks to generate positive impact through empathy and partnering with others, which is especially true for whom they deem to be their 'customers'. There is a clear bias for allowing the entire ecosystem to naturally become more cohesive and harmonious both within and without while being open to any amount of change at any given time. This stage is the equivalent to what Frederic Laloux's *Reinventing Organizations* refers to as the stage at which we see the emergence of 'Teal' Organizations which are organizations that 'sense' what their needs are and where the organization itself is organically growing and evolving.

The paradigm of the Intuitive stage has direct parallels to what is widely believed to be the next stage in the evolution of human consciousness. This paradigm views the organization as an independent force with its own purpose, and not merely as a vehicle for achieving management's objectives. The company sees itself as being in service to the world and humanity, which is a next-level expansion of servant leadership that began to emerge in the Purposeful stage and took hold internally in the Transparent stage.

Intuitive organizations are characterized by self-organization and self-management, further building on the deep trust and transparency established at the prior level. Individuals may assume a multiplicity of roles that are self-selected and highly fluid. They go where they are needed and contribute to the best of their abilities. For everyone across the organization this stage is reflected in a completely ego-free environment where there is an absolute minimization of any feeling or 'need' to control, fit in or 'look good' in front of others. The fear that lives underneath all of those behaviors has been overcome and left behind. Taming the fears of the ego unlocks the power of true intuition as the higher vantage point reached at this level allows one to see the world with a broader perspective. This is why this stage highlights so many parallels to our evolving human consciousness. Looking back over the progression through the initial stages, the shift to Connected happens when Surviving internalizes rules that allow it to disidentify from impulsively satisfying its needs. The shift to Confident happens when

Connected disidentifies from group norms. At this stage, the shift from Transparent to Intuitive happens through the disidentification from the ego. Having gone 'beyond' the ego allows people to see how fears, ambitions, and desires have been running their lives. At this stage there is no longer a complete fusion with the ego so there are no longer situations where fear reflexively controls behavior. In the process, space is created where people can listen to the wisdom of other, deeper parts of themselves and the company. Following the collective intuition is the primary guidance for all organizations, teams, and people at this stage.

For the self-managing organization, the hierarchical "predict and control" mentality that at one time permeated all processes and funding models has been replaced with a decentralized structure consisting of small teams that take responsibility for their own governance and for how they interact with other parts of the organization. All processes and procedures are based on non-linear peer interactions using simple rules and guiding principles. Meetings are rare and decisions are no longer made by those with 'authority' because everyone is empowered and trusted to make their own decisions. Everyone in the company trusts their 'inner rightness' when making decisions knowing that what they choose will be true to their purpose and is serving the world. The use of an 'advice' process allows collaboration and communication to help an individual make the best decisions possible while a 'conflict resolution' process helps people raise and address issues effectively and with psychological safety.

Assigned positions and job descriptions are no longer helpful given the wide variety and fluidity of roles that people may assume at any given time. People's actions are guided not by orders from someone up the chain of command but by 'listening' to the organization's purpose. If a problem or opportunity exists people will share that information and immediately take the initiative to address it. This immediacy results in frequent small adjustments that keep issues from snowballing. Unlike the highly static nature of Connected, Confident and Purposeful organizations, the organizational structure of the Intuitive company is characterized by these rapid changes and adaptations, as adjustments are continuously made to better serve the organization's ever-changing purpose. This stage represents the ultimate ideal of the Agile movement, where all efforts, both business and technology, deal with adversity quickly and gracefully.

The skills and technologies seen in an Intuitive organization directly reflect the ideas behind complex adaptive systems. The internet itself is an example of a CAS having an immense number of related but different elements with intricate relationships and interconnections. Within a given company at this level, networking and 'systems of systems' are used both in providing solutions as well as how people and teams interact and share information regarding tools and techniques. At this stage there is no distinction between 'business strategy' and 'enterprise architecture' as the focus has shifted to finding better ways to serve the organization's unique sense of evolutionary purpose, rather than out-think the competition. Just as all team members are encouraged to "listen" for opportunities and test these via the advice process, technology efforts take the same approach by discussing emerging needs and opportunities with other skilled and knowledgeable colleagues where there is no organizational distinction between 'the business' and IT. In this environment every single person has become an innovator and a problem solver. In prior stages product innovation was commonly associated with exhaustive analyses of customer segments, buyer behaviors, and the competition, which is a very analytical 'left-brain' approach. In the Intuitive company, the source of innovation engages the creative 'right brain' that is driven by purpose and 'listens' for what seem to be the right solutions. These organizations look to build products and solutions they will be proud of, that will fill a genuine need in the world, and that they are uniquely capable of providing. Design Thinking and Ideation approaches truly shine in these companies, as these types of structured design practices are specifically intended to catalyze empathetic thinking. Frontline workers may spend long periods out in the field observing how their customers are using their products and services and they are free to act on insights gained from working closely with the customer. The drive for continuous learning and adaptation creates a deep understanding of customer needs. With everyone being entirely self-managing, there is nothing to keep a good idea from being pursued if it has use for customers and if its pursuit adheres to the advice process. New insights and practices are systematically shared through the organization through tools that mimic a social network or social media, including communal code sharing and open-source approaches using tools such as GitHub. Through the experimentation and accelerated learning that supports an evolutionary purpose, innovations that prove to be successful are shared and adopted quickly throughout the organization. In true ecological and symbiotic fashion, emergent innovations do not just follow the organizational purpose, they may also impact the evolutionary purpose of the organization itself by shifting toward a new direction and potential. At this stage, the so-called 'Enterprise Architecture' is fluid and in a constant state of evolution, modernization, and transformation. The technologies of Intuitive organizations are part of a dynamic ecosystem, as well as a dynamic ecosystem unto themselves. This is directly in line with the emerging use of artificial intelligence, advanced analytics and machine learning. Anything that allows an organization to sense and adapt in real time is at the heart of a complex adaptive system.

Those that work as part of an Intuitive organization may have notably different views on what should be rewarded and recognized. These companies openly celebrate rapid learning, even when that learning was a 'failure' or a mistake. This reinforces the notion that everyone is both trusted to do what they believe is right, and safe to experiment and innovate without fear. Employees are in pursuit of a life well-lived and other rewards and recognition are secondary to that objective (although they readily admit that those secondary rewards are capable of facilitating 'pleasurable experiences'!). The Intuitive stage has shifted the worldview from one of scarcity and fear to one of abundance and trust. Although rare in today's world, abundance economies and 'gift cultures' do exist that reflect these same values where status and recognition are functions of what you give away, not how much you control. Reputation among peer groups is the measure of success in an abundance economy. An example of this can be directly seen in the open-source community where code is not a scarce resource and one's level of recognition is based on what they have contributed to the community for its use and wellbeing. Everyone is contributing to the survival, evolution, and success of the overall entity without any demands for compensation.

At the Intuitive stage, the guiding metaphor has become one where the organization is seen as a living system or living organism. Life, in all its evolutionary wisdom, manages ecosystems of unfathomable beauty, ever evolving toward more wholeness, complexity, and consciousness and an Intuitive organization is one of those ecosystems. Change in nature happens everywhere, all the time, in a self-organizing urge that comes from every cell and every organism, with no need for central command and control to give orders or pull the levers. Evolution continues to march onward and upward and none of us knows exactly what things will look like when we transcend our current levels of being.

Transcendent

The Transcendent stage is a future phase that goes above and beyond what we are currently capable of conceiving as 'work' and 'life' in any detailed fashion. Taking the Intuitive stage's understanding that we are on a journey of personal and collective unfolding toward our true nature, and also considering that all of the stages up to this point have been an integral part of this continued unfolding, there is a definite trajectory that can give us some early hints and insights to where this next stage of organizational evolution may be headed.

In looking at both that trajectory as well as various wisdom traditions we can craft a rough outline of what this stage may hold for the future. The Transcendent stage will in all likelihood be characterized as pure selfless service to the world and humanity that is guided with humility and focused on making a significant contribution to future generations. To the Transcendent level organization, operating holistically and experientially will be second nature and normal matter of course. This constitutes an integral state where all actions and behaviors incorporate both synthesis and renewal, i.e., the 'taking in' from the surrounding environment and immediately using that to create something new and valuable. This represents an operation with a sense of pure awareness that breaks down and begins to invalidate the IMT quadrant differentiations of internal, external, individual, and collective as it drives toward "freedom from all the structures by their transparent rearrangement into one integral Oneness of being"[20].

For the Transcendent organization, 'operating experientially' may mean that processes and budgets are effectively things of the past. In the same way that the 'Ri' stage of Shu-Ha-Ri brings martial arts students to the state of mastery where "we completely depart from the forms, open the door to creative technique, and arrive in a place where we act in accordance with what our heart/mind desires, unhindered while not overstepping laws"[21], the Transcendent organization will have no need for the 'forms' of pre-defined processes and budgets. The technologies and the people that create them may also be 'becoming one'. As Yuval Noah Harari explores in his books *"Sapiens"* and *"Homo Deus: A Brief History of Tomorrow"*[22], advances in biotechnologies, such as gene editing methods like CRISPR, while at the same time advances continue to occur in artificial intelligence and machine learning, organizations may soon be building brain-computer interfaces that will blur the line between man and machine. As humans we may be evolving into a combination of the biological and the technological, not just using technology but integrating technology into our bodies. It is an open question as to what lies in the future. Does the Transcendent organization achieve some form of unification or blending between 'company' and 'customer'? Who knows?

Another very intriguing concept is that in this stage of consciousness, which presumably already exists in a handful of people today, there is an ability to perceive time and space as an integrated whole. Instead of being locked into a fixed past, present, and/or future, a three-dimensional universe, or a self that is divided into categories, these people can experience time, space, and mind in terms of their overall effect on life and destiny. As Harari has posited,

"The way we understand space and time may also change. Today we have organic bodies, hence at any one time, we can be only in one place. But a future cyborg may have an organic brain connected via a brain-computer interface to numerous arms, legs, and other tools that could be scattered all over the world. Your brain could be in New York, while your hands will be fighting insurgents in Afghanistan or performing heart surgery in Egypt. So where are you?".

As organizations build even further upon the shift to abundance economies and 'gift culture', we may also see the advent of Transcendent companies that find specific rewards and recognition to be unnecessary. As values, belief systems and experience are expected to show them, the universe will take care of the organization, its people, and its customers and they will automatically receive like value for the value they provide others.

The Transcendent stage can give us may interesting ideas to ponder, but at this point it is mostly conjecture and not directly relevant to what we know today as Modernization and Transformation initiatives. Yet what it does provide is an upper boundary to the IMT maturity scale and a sense of directionality as to where business and certain types of organizations may be headed to in the future. It is a reminder that evolution is ongoing – and it isn't done with us yet!

Putting the Aspect & Stage Pieces Together

Using the descriptions of the seven stages, it is possible to approximate where a particular organization might fall on the maturity continuum as a whole. Yet in the true nature of holons, the maturity levels described above also apply equally to each of the four aspects contained within the IMT quadrant model (Individual, Cultural, Environmental, and Organizational) in terms of what stage each of them is functioning at within the overall organization. Each aspect may in fact be operating from markedly different levels of maturity. Therefore, if in our diagrammatic representation we consider the intersection of the interior/exterior and individual/collective lines to be the 'origin', then the maturity level relative to each quadrant can be depicted as having progressed away from the origin to a certain stage:

Knowing that each stage includes and transcends the previous stages, it is imperative to keep in mind that some of the characteristics of earlier stages continue to be necessary in order to function effectively at higher levels and that those characteristics may come to the surface under certain circumstances. Understanding at what stage each aspect is operating under 'normal' circumstances can help prevent the over or under estimation of where each aspect currently lands on the maturity continuum. The risk to making an accurate assessment arises when there is an attempt to deny or 'disown' any of the less-desirable characteristics of those earlier stages. It is common to believe that growth and maturation have occurred when in fact the underlying behaviors and mindsets have not truly changed or evolved at all. Without acknowledging, integrating, and transcending the traits of prior stages, a Modernization or Transformation effort, and possibly the entire organization itself, will eventually fail.

In the preceding sections there were several different types of characteristics used to describe each stage of maturity. When looking more closely at the pieces of this puzzle that are represented by a combination of IMT quadrants and stages, a realization occurs that each one of these combinations is actually made up of many smaller pieces that correspond to these specific types of characteristics. There is a puzzle that exists within the puzzle of assessing levels of maturity. Therefore, we need to expand this model further so that we can identify the remaining pieces that will show us where we are at a more granular level, which will subsequently allow us to identify specific areas where we might be 'stuck' in modernizing or transforming any of the aspects of the organization.

Little Pieces - Developmental Lines

Every individual piece in a jigsaw puzzle has multiple characteristics such as its size, shape, color, thickness, gloss, and orientation. It is only through the analysis and assessment of all of the characteristics of a given piece that we can figure out exactly where that piece fits in the overall puzzle. Once placed, that piece helps to narrow down some of the attributes necessary in the adjacent pieces that still need to be found and placed. The same holds true for each of the four IMT aspects in that there are multiple characteristics common to each quadrant that will show more specific levels of relative maturity and progress.

Before we can make a sound determination of which stage each quadrant is operating from, we need to assess these more specific traits and behaviors that will provide us with the detailed information necessary. When attempting to gauge the maturity of any of the four quadrants we must consider the value systems in play that influence behavior, the perceived needs that drive motivation, the structures provided through processes and budgets, the technologies and skill sets that exist, and how recognition and rewards are viewed and leveraged. Each of these characteristics has an influence on each individual, each team, each working environment, and the organization overall. Oftentimes the actual maturity level is not only a composite of these characteristics, but it also reflects the 'reality' of the entity in question which may not always line up with what it believes, wishes, or publicly touts itself to be. Ask any employee if they believe their company is living up to its stated mission and values, and you'll get the truth about how close to these ideals they are actually operating. This assumes the employees are aware of what the company mission and values are!

To assist in determining the stage of maturity from which each aspect is operating, and in turn, where Modernization and Transformation efforts can have the most immediate and lasting effect, the IMT nested quadrant model (see <u>Interlocking Aspects – Pieces of Pieces</u> above) can be expanded by defining and inserting multiple 'developmental lines' within each quadrant[23]. These lines represent traits that both influence and reflect the many smaller and nuanced variations in maturity that exist for anything being assessed. The IMT model's Developmental Lines are as follows:

- Values & Common Understanding
- Needs & Identity
- Processes & Budgeting
- Skills & Technology
- Rewards & Recognition

These lines of development exist whether we are talking about an individual employee, a team, a working environment, or the organization overall. Each line in any quadrant of any entity may have a different level of maturity and therefore the uniqueness of that entity in its own context can be captured and visualized in a fairly detailed fashion. Exactly *how* we determine the level of maturity for any given line is driven by the categorization of interior vs exterior and individual vs collective for the entity being assessed. Personal (individual) and Cultural (team) maturity will be evaluated through identifying what the people *think, feel, and believe* about each line of development, while Employment (environmental) and Organizational aspects will be measured based on empirical evidence – i.e., that which can be *seen, heard, and touched.* In the sections below we will give a description of each developmental line and the characteristics typically shown at each stage of maturity, but it is helpful at this point to visualize these lines of development in combination with the stages of maturity described in the prior section. Combining all lines and stages into a grid we get the following diagrammatic representation:

	Values and Common Understanding	Needs and Identity	Process and Budgeting	Skills and Technology	Rewards and Recognition
Transcendent	Experiential	Service	Freeform	Leading Edge	Unnecessary
Intuitive	Experimental	Mastery	Adaptive	Dynamic	Life well lived
Transparent	Truth	Autonomy	Light Weight	Integrated	EE Experience
Purposeful	People	Purpose	Products	Components	Intrinsic
Confident	Profit	Achievement	Projects	Proven S	Heroism
Connected	Group	Role Clarity	Compliance	Proven SSS	Merit / Rank
Surviving	Self	Power & SSS	Ad-Hoc	Available	Loyalty/None

This grid provides the framework for a graphical method by which we can plot the current state or envision a possible future state for any individual, team, employment environment, or organizational environment. An assessment can be made, through any number of various methods (many of which are detailed in the Connecting the Pieces section below) that help to identify where the subject in question currently falls in terms of maturity on each developmental line. Assessment results can be depicted as a bar graph that captures a moment in time for that given entity.

To illustrate the concept with an example, let's say that we are creating a chart for a particular individual who is a software developer for Company X. Although there are four quadrants that will provide us a complete picture for this individual, the first step is to assess the Personal quadrant, meaning we want to understand this person's beliefs about themselves while at work. Through the use of multiple assessment techniques, it is determined that this individual is one who thinks, feels, and believes the following:

1. My decisions and priorities are consistently made in favor of what is the most profitable for Company X (Values & Common Understanding)
2. I believe my purpose is clear, and that is to provide a quality product that meets a specific need for the company's customers (Needs & Identity)
3. I believe that there are clear expectations for all Company X developers (such as myself), and that each of us must remain

strictly compliant with all documented processes, delivering scope commitments on time and under budget with no exceptions (Process & Budgeting)

4. I think I have the right skills to work with the proven (yet expensive) technologies that have been in use by the company for a long time (Skills & Technology)

5. I feel the way to earn rewards is by consistently showing loyalty and allegiance to my superiors (Rewards & Recognition)

Therefore, a developmental lines bar chart generated for this individual representing the current state of the Personal quadrant might look something like this:

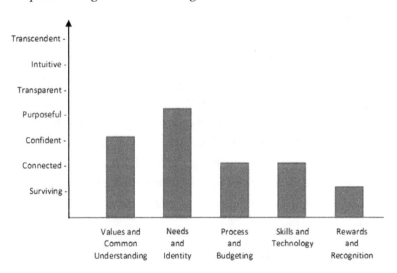

Remember that for this individual, this graph represents what they *think, feel, and believe* about themselves with regards to their work. The 'reality' through someone else's eyes might be very different but for this particular person it accurately reflects their internal perceptions and, as is the case for any individual, perception *is* reality. That is why generating several of these diagrams for each quadrant of the IMT model for individuals, teams, employment environments and the organization itself will help to gain a true understanding of the pieces we have to work with that will be contributing to the final solution of our puzzle. For our hypothetical employee, if the leadership team of Company X believes they are about to wrap up a successful Agile Transformation, but the IMT charts generated for the employees reveal a majority of the people on the delivery teams believe, just as this person does, that they are driven to 'deliver scope commitments on time and under budget without question' then there is a clear disconnect that needs to be addressed because those beliefs are counter to Agile values and principles. By identifying the divide that exists, specific strategies and tactics to address the disconnect can be added to the Transformation program plan itself to mitigate this risk of failure and also enable further growth and maturity. That said, below are descriptions of each developmental line that can be used to determine and capture the relative level of maturity of any given entity.

Values & Common Understanding

The Values & Common Understanding line of development represents the belief system that exists between and amongst the leaders and employees of an organization. The common understanding of what a company values is different, sometimes significantly, from what an organization may publish and communicate as it's company or 'core' values. The true value system and culture at work within an organization is what drives the company to do what it does, how it does it, and how people in the organization behave. This developmental line provides an answer to the question *"What am I aware of?"* which in turn lays bare a common understanding of whatever ethos permeates all individuals, teams, environments, and the organization overall.

This line also addresses the question *"What is significant to me?"*, where an understanding of what people and companies find to be meaningful and important can help ascertain the relative level of maturity for this line. A little bit of moral assessment might come into play when answering this question because we may be determining if people are doing whatever they are told in order to get special favors and rewards (or to avoid punishment and retribution), or if they are choosing to do what is 'right'. The relative level of customer-centricity is also a key contributor when assessing the maturity of this line. The level to which the customer is front of mind will reveal what is deemed to be significant or important, as there are varying levels of how much focus, care and respect is being provided to customers.

To assess the level of maturity that exists for the Values & Common Understanding developmental line, the table below provides a high-level description of the primary concerns (values, priorities, and behaviors) that align and correspond with each stage of maturity:

Stage	Concerns
Surviving	Self, 'Me'; Relative power rank (dominate or submit); Exploitation; Doing *only* what told to do
Connected	Group or team, 'Us'; Conformity; Avoidance of spotlight and punishment
Confident	Profitability, achievement, and expertise; Work done thoroughly and scientifically
Purposeful	People, community, empathy, 'We'; Teamwork, collaboration, tolerance
Transparent	Truth, open and honest communication; Integrity and authenticity; Meaning and creativity
Intuitive	Experimental, empathetic, adaptive; Open to change; Serving the world and humanity
Transcendent	Experiential; Unfolding journey; Unitive and Holistic; Abundance; Future Generations

In looking at the Values & Common Understanding developmental line in a more detailed fashion across the stages of maturity, we can see how each of the key concerns listed above describe different value systems that come with their own inherent beliefs and behaviors. As awareness grows value systems evolve and change, allowing the limitations of a particular stage to be overcome and transcended through a broader worldview and the ability to handle increased levels of complexity.

The core values of the Surviving stage are inherently ego-centric, exploitative, and impulsive. The worldview is that the world is hostile and dangerous, and only the strongest and mightiest survive while the weak serve the strong. It is the stage of 'Me' that results in an 'every man for himself' set of behaviors. Operating with an animalistic wolfpack mentality, each individual is asserting themselves in the name of dominance, conquest, and power. They want what they want, and they want it *now*. This is the level of immediate gratification, battles of will, and public displays of power. Organizational relationships and structures are heavily political, power driven, and top-down with the 'strongest' on top. Those of the 'weaker' lower ranks are exploited for the benefit of the 'strong' and will do exactly what they are told to do, and nothing more.

At the Connected stage, the impetuousness and impulsiveness of the power struggle seen at the Survival stage is overcome by the emergence of a set of strong bonds forged with groups and teams brought together around a common belief. These groups see value in order, structure, stability, and conformity to the *'one'* right way of doing things. Those that conform are rewarded while those that do not are publicly punished and ostracized, which in turn reinforces the 'Us versus Them' mentality. Absolute obedience to rules and authority figures is expected while roles and responsibilities are explicit and well-defined. Organizational relationships and structures are hierarchical, bureaucratic, and based on seniority.

As groups begin to question how they can get better at what they do (going beyond was previously blindly believed to be the *'one'* right way), they enter the Confident stage. Putting profit above all else, the push at this stage is to grow to a larger scale using scientific methods to become more efficient at both operations and wealth generation. The world is seen as full of possibilities to make things better and bring prosperity. Achievement and expertise are highly valued and trusted as they are seen as key characteristics that will identify and use all available opportunities and resources to reach and exceed the defined goals. Organizational relationships and structures are all based around profit-generation (i.e., increasing shareholder value), competition, and innovation.

After achieving the material benefits of the Confident stage, a realization begins to set in that there is more to life than individual fame and fortune. A deeper sense of community and empathy begin to highlight the values emerging at the Purposeful stage. This stage puts people over profit, as the belief is that the world is a shared habitat where everyone can find purpose and meaning. This level values equality, community, and empathy which are all linked to the idea of 'We' in a global sense which fully supplants the 'Us versus Them' mentality that originated at the Connected stage. Teamwork, collaboration, and tolerance take hold at the Purposeful stage which includes newfound consideration for individual feelings and emotions. Organizational relationships and structures add a 'bottom-up' component to what was previously a 'top-down only' approach, creating more equality, empowerment, and dedication in contributing to a larger purpose.

Fully leaving behind the various inhibiting structures inherent in all of the previous stages, the Transparent stage removes the veil and reveals the values of leading a more meaningful and authentic existence. A dedication to speaking truth at all times through open and honest communication becomes the hallmark of this stage. All actions are taken with integrity and authenticity and seek to uncover increasingly deeper meaning through creative functions. Identifying individual strengths and aptitudes allows for those strengths to be further developed and leveraged for better collective outcomes.

After getting in touch with an 'authentic self' at the Transparent stage, a new way of interacting with the world in an Intuitive way emerges. Organizations, people, and the world are all seen as various levels of complex adaptive systems (CAS) where experimentation, empathy, and openness to change are highly valued. Being able to adapt in response to what is unfolding all around us allows us to better serve the world and humanity. At this stage it is understood that this journey is continuing to unfold, which is leading us to evolve in sync with 'all that is' until the next level of Transcendent existence arrives.

Needs & Identity

The Needs & Identity developmental line asks, not all that surprisingly, "*What do I need?*". This line is ultimately about underlying motives and motivations, which are not necessarily one and the same thing. Beyond the absolute survival needs of food, water, and shelter, all other so-called needs are based on changing perceptions. The reasons behind what spurs people to action in order to fulfill a perceived need are the *motives*, while *motivation* is the energy that goes into performing those actions.

When actions generate positive results, then there is an increase in motivation to continue pursuing even more actions and more positive results. Therefore, by understanding what causes people, teams, or organizations to act with noticeable drive and enthusiasm (motivation), we begin to understand what they believe they 'need' (motives). Motives are primarily the social and psychological reasons behind why we do things such as go to work or engage in certain relationships, all of which are ways in which we expect to meet our needs. By having our needs met, we are more at ease, feel a sense of comfort, and feel that life is good. When we come across someone who feels like their needs are being met, this also gives us direct insight into who they believe they are or should be.

Consequently, the Needs & Identity line also asks, "*Who am I?*" This is how one sees oneself relative to the larger environment, i.e., how one believes one fits into the bigger picture. The self-identity of individuals, teams, leadership, or the organization will directly reflect each one's level of maturity. Does the CEO believe herself to be the strong and dominant 'Alpha' leader? Does the company take pride in being a collection of distinguished scientific experts? Looking at the table below, the concerns listed for each stage of maturity help to determine the appropriate assessment for this developmental line:

Stage	Concerns
Surviving	Safety and security; Money and benefits; Power
Connected	Role clarity and belonging (fitting in)

Stage	Concerns
Confident	Success, knowledge, distinction; Self-esteem
Purposeful	Acceptance, empowerment, compassion, feeling; Seeking purpose
Transparent	Autonomy, trust; Highlight strengths; Living purpose
Intuitive	Mastery and personal growth; Evolutionary purpose
Transcendent	Selfless Service

At the Surviving stage, the main concerns are with safety and security, which includes personal, emotional, and financial security. The undeniable physiological needs of food, water, clothing, shelter, and physical health must be met, and in a business context the way these needs are met comes about through the continued pursuit of money and benefits. Job security and the maintenance of current lifestyle are paramount at this level because *not* having these needs met is truly a direct threat to continued survival. The way people tend to go about obtaining and retaining their job and lifestyle, which also speaks to their perceived psychological and emotional needs, is through the exertion of raw personal power over others. At the Surviving stage it is believed that by increasing power there is a much better chance that all material needs will be met.

Once basic survival needs have been met, there is a shift in needs at the Connected stage toward a sense of belonging that is found through relationships with like-minded people. The same sense of family and friendship that is sought outside the workplace is replicated on the job when seeking to 'fit in' by finding a well-defined position with clear roles and responsibilities. When placed into a group where everyone has clear job duties, a sense of comfort is found through social acceptance and conformity by doing what is expected.

After establishing a strong sense of belonging and social acceptance, attention again turns inward when seeking an improved sense of self-esteem at the Confident stage. Pursuing success, knowledge and distinction are driven by this new need to receive recognition from others. It results in striving to be known as an achiever or an expert, gaining status and prestige, which in turn feeds the perceived need by improving the internal sense of worth and confidence in certain abilities.

At the Purposeful level, the sense of self-esteem matures into something more in tune with emotions and feelings rather than external recognition and material success. Seeking more personal acceptance and empowerment, this level has a need for equality and compassion for all human beings, especially those that are in direct relationship with each other. The goal is to find a purpose or calling that has a clear resonance.

Once a true purpose is uncovered, the Transparent stage seeks to fully embrace and live that purpose. By playing to natural strengths and inborn gifts, the motivation that comes to the forefront is to align with one's purpose in the best possible way. This level is driven to be completely truthful, open, and honest in all communications when pursuing that purpose, which establishes an additional need for trust. Being able to trust oneself and others is at the root of the associated need for autonomy and independence characteristic of this stage.

Once purpose and autonomy are well established, needs again expand to seek a sense of mastery in what one does. Growth in both depth and breadth of skills, capabilities, and interests are actively sought after at the Intuitive stage. By pursuing greater knowledge and wisdom it becomes easier to align with and pursue an ever-changing purpose in life. This evolutionary purpose will lead to the need to provide selfless service to the world and humanity at the Transcendent stage.

Processes & Budgeting

The Processes & Budgeting developmental line is the first of two 'kinesthetic' lines, with the second being Skills & Technology. When combined they answer the question "*How should I physically do this?*". Therefore, the actual 'concerns' that drive how things get done at each stage are consistent across both lines while the 'results' are the direct outcomes that come from prioritizing a given concern. For Processes & Budgeting, those relationships can be seen in the assessment table below:

Stage	Concerns / Results
Surviving	Immediacy; Ad-Hoc and Haphazard
Connected	Risk Avoidance; Rigid Compliance
Confident	Profitable and Predictable; Project-Driven
Purposeful	Customer-centric; Product-Driven
Transparent	Optimization; Lean and Efficient
Intuitive	Adaptive; Agile and Nimble
Transcendent	Next Generation; Freeform

At the Surviving stage, the need for immediate gratification results in attitudes of 'just do it' and 'git 'er done', taking the approach of doing whatever it takes to get the job done as soon as possible and with minimal financial controls. This frequently results in there being no structure or safety net for those doing the work. The Capability Maturity Model (CMM) describes this 'Initial' stage of process maturity as 'ad-hoc'[24] because it is completely haphazard in nature due to the characteristic short-sightedness of the Surviving stage itself. It is the stage where success is heavily dependent on the heroics of individuals and can rarely, if ever, be replicated. This stage is naturally and consistently chaotic due to the lack of clear processes and budget structures.

Moving to the Connected stage typically happens as a result of the painful lessons learned during the Surviving stage. Having been burned in the past, there is a significant aversion to risk that emerges at this level and, as a result, processes and budgets become inherently rigid and deterministic. These become the communicated constraints encapsulating a belief that if they are followed to the letter then success is guaranteed. Expecting absolute conformity to the process with a command-and-control attitude of "this is how we do it here" becomes the impetus for a strict set of roles, responsibilities, and handoffs. This is the level of bureaucratic 'red tape'. Waterfall delivery approaches originate at this level and give rise to the need for Project Managers, prescriptive Software Development Life Cycles (SDLC), and the like.

As profitability concerns start to outweigh some of the extreme aversion to risk, the Confident stage expands into a more well-established project management approach focused on being 'on-time' and 'under-budget'. Focusing on the project management 'Iron Triangle' variables of cost, time, and scope, detailed estimates and predicted timelines and deadlines receive the most time and attention. Status reports consistently use the RAG format (Red, Amber/Yellow, Green) where the project's color is determined by assessing if the effort itself is on-time and under-budget (Green) or some pre-determined percentage of 'off-plan' (Yellow or Red). Processes and budgets dictate that corrective actions must be taken to get a project 'back to green' per the original plan. This is also the stage where a 'scientific' approach to 'resource utilization' results in the wide use of allocation spreadsheets that set a value for how much time each person is to spend on each project they are assigned to, all based on the various estimates generated across all projects. The goal is to maximize productivity and ensure 100% utilization of every person concurrently keeping all projects 'on track'.

Upon realizing the inherent myopia of the project-driven approach, the Purposeful stage entails a move to focusing on *products* over *projects*. Units of work may still get completed within something of a 'project' container set of constraints (i.e., an allocation of funds based on scope), but the sequence of 'projects' is now related to the evolution of a valuable product or 'value stream'. Operating at this stage is also seen in a shift from tracking resource utilization across projects to more stable and long-lived teams that have a common purpose. Aligning the product mindset with dedicated teams provides for more customer-centricity in how solutions are developed and how subsequent customer needs and usage drive further investment and development.

Still seeking to provide solutions better, faster, and cheaper, the Transparent stage embraces Lean principles and practices to search for efficiencies at every turn. This requires exposing the truth of what is actually happening on the ground in the name of transparency. Optimization cannot occur without bringing all of the empirical evidence to light.

By accelerating learning through optimization, rapid change and adaptation becomes possible. Growing from a realization that the future cannot be predicted or controlled in any fashion, true Agility becomes the main characteristic of the Intuitive stage of maturity for Processes and Budgeting. This is the acknowledgement that the company operates in what the Cynefin decision-making framework refers to as the 'Complex' domain where 'unknown unknowns' mean cause and effect can only be deduced after the fact[25]. Only through a process of experimental probing, sensing, and responding will effective solutions and behaviors emerge. By integrating the Lean aspects characteristic of the prior Transparent stage, learning becomes accelerated which in turn drives more frequent 'pivot or persevere' decisions as the findings of various experiments continue to come to light. The resulting nature is one that is elegantly adaptive to what unfolds over the passage of time.

As evolution continues, the mere concepts of processes and budgets may come into question as to whether or not they are valid forms of operating. In the same spirit of the martial arts concept of Shu-Ha-Ri mentioned earlier, next generation approaches may very well move 'beyond all forms' of processes and budgets, incorporating them as tools that are applied only if and when necessary. The Transcendent stage will be something above and beyond what we know today, perhaps a Zen-like one where 'the process is that there is no process', yet without the unknowledgeable, unwise, and haphazard approach of where it all started in the ad-hoc Surviving stage.

Skills & Technologies

The Skills & Technologies developmental line is the second 'Kinesthetic' line that tells us *"How should I physically do this?"*. In the same way that Processes & Budgeting have results at each stage that are driven by corresponding concerns, the Skills & Technologies line is also a direct reflection of what is deemed to be important at each stage of maturity. Those stage-specific priorities will also be reflected in the relative level of competency, capabilities, and talents that become embedded in the people, processes, tools, and technologies themselves. The assessment table for the Skills & Technologies developmental line contains the following:

Stage	Concerns / Results
Surviving	Immediacy; Readily Available
Connected	Risk Avoidance; Proven (costly)
Confident	Profitable and Predictable; Proven (cheap)

Stage	Concerns /Results
Purposeful	Customer-centric; Best Fit Components
Transparent	Optimization; Integrated and Unified
Intuitive	Adaptive; Dynamic Ecosystems
Transcendent	Next Generation; Leading/Bleeding Edge Innovations

The drive for immediate gratification at the Surviving stage, and the impulsive nature of that stage overall, leads to the ad-hoc use of whatever technologies are readily available using whatever skill sets already exist in-house. Given the haphazardness, there is virtually no such thing as an Enterprise Architecture approach to solutioning or operations. Chaos reigns at this level with a constant state of disorganization and lack of predictability. There is no cohesion between the minimal IT infrastructure and business operations. Everything is reactive, issues and their responses are unpredictable, and standards are not developed for how to resolve problems. The lack of trust between groups is also reflected in a lack of trust in the siloed data that exists across their disparate and separate systems.

The risk aversion that comes to be at the Connected stage frequently leads to the creation of an 'Ivory Tower' Enterprise Architecture group, with their extensive modeling and documentation of the 'as-is' and 'to-be' state of all things IT. The EA team works in relative isolation and has the authority to enforce the strict use of all of their recommendations, standards, and implementation requirements by all other development and delivery teams. The architecture is effectively 'monolithic' and the technologies in use are slow to change, as 'tried-and-true' solutions remain in use regardless of age or cost (old mainframe solutions and COBOL code are a couple of great examples). The skill sets that exist are directly driven by what is approved by Enterprise Architecture, which is typically captured in extensive models based on the Zachman Framework or TOGAF. The conformity to these well-documented standards is the perceived way to minimize technological and business risk.

The Confident stage sees the advent of an Enterprise Architecture that is not quite as stagnant or rigid as seen in the Connected stage. Taking a more scientific approach to improving capabilities while leveraging the expertise that is concurrently emerging, Enterprise Architects begin to search for solutions that, while still relatively low risk, can help contribute to revenue generation and cost-cutting objectives. Enterprise Architecture skills also move closer to development and delivery skills as the emergence of the Solutions Architect and Technical Architect roles help put EA models and theory into practice and implementation. While the various technology roles and skills move closer to each other, there is still a distinct separation between 'the Business' and IT, where defining and building solutions happens in a requirements-heavy 'order maker, order taker' fashion. Skill sets begin to become more diverse at this stage but are still very much determined by the overall Enterprise Architecture approach which retains much of its monolithic nature and preference for well proven, albeit cheaper technologies.

The Purposeful level goes beyond the internal back-and-forth negotiations between 'the Business' and IT to become much more oriented around coming together to build valuable products that better meet customer needs. The result is an Enterprise Architecture group that is focused on collaborating with both business and technology colleagues to provide guidance and insight. The Enterprise Architecture itself is now being built around a set of diversified technologies that are highly componentized and create a number of 'best-fit' solutions, thereby becoming much less monolithic in nature. Multiple technologies are used to create and support multiple products and customer channels. The skill sets required to support this diverse set of componentized solutions leads to people developing "T-shaped" skills that, while having a more varied set of generalized skills, also provides for specific individuals to develop deep expertise in a few key areas. The combined sets of skills across teams create both depth and breadth of skills that eliminates the risk of having single points of failure. Enterprise Architecture functions at the Purposeful stage are pushed down to the team level, eliminating the need for a clear distinction between Architects and Tech Leads in general. This level significantly expands the use of data and analytics to concurrently support internal decision making and a unified cross-platform customer experience.

The Transparent stage expands on the level of customer-centric technologies as the complete set of solutions is intended to now provide a unified and transparent omnichannel customer experience. Enterprise Architectures shift to fully integrated and unified sets of fit-for-purpose solutions that communicate with each other through application program interfaces (APIs) and shared data. Microservice architectures replace SOA skills enabling business capabilities with automated deployments, intelligent endpoints, and decentralized control of functions and data. Technology solutions that provide self-healing and self-scaling capabilities provide the needed performance and stability required to meet varying levels of customer usage and demand, as this contributes directly to the overall customer experience and business continuity. Given the interconnected nature of these architectures, the skill sets required on a per person basis expand significantly to address combined ownership of development, testing, architecture, infrastructure management, and operations. At the Transparent stage, the Enterprise Architecture is inherently more capable of supporting both business and technical agility needs.

True agility arrives with the Intuitive stage given its equivalence to a complex adaptive system (CAS), as technology architectures expand to an immense number of related but different elements with intricate relationships and interconnections. Networks and 'systems of systems' are common themes across solutions, tools, and techniques. Enterprise Architecture is itself a clear reflection of the current business strategy and provides the necessary adaptability and nimbleness because any component at any degree of granularity can be modified or replaced easily and with minimal lead times and operational impacts. This allows technology to be yet another reflection of a continuously evolving organizational purpose. In the Intuitive company, purpose-driven innovative solutions emerge from a general openness to change, the sharing of knowledge and advice between technology people, and an experimental approach used to identify what works and what doesn't. There is a minimalist nature to technology and architecture at this stage as well, as nothing exists that is extraneous or does not directly contribute to addressing a genuine need in the world. Because knowledge and skills are constantly evolving, techniques, insights, practices, tools and code are systematically shared throughout the organization through social networks. The technology environments of Intuitive organizations are dynamic ecosystems that leverage the use of rapid learning technologies such as artificial intelligence, advanced analytics, and machine learning to sense and adapt in real time.

As technology continues to progress and become closer and closer to being fully integrated with humans themselves, the Transcendent phase may bring any number of next-generation breakthroughs and disruptors that constantly push the envelope of what is considered 'leading' or 'bleeding' edge technologies. A unique intrigue lies behind those terms, as they have the potential for entirely new, and much more literal meanings as we continue down our evolutionary path.

Rewards & Recognition
The Rewards & Recognition developmental line asks the question, *"How am I best supported?"*. When engaging in work with

others there are associated expectations of how to behave. At each stage of maturity these expectations change, yet across all stages, if specific behaviors are adequately displayed then they are recognized and rewarded accordingly. There is a feeling of being supported that results when displaying expected behaviors as well as when seeing corresponding behaviors in other people. Therefore, the Rewards & Recognition developmental line has the following support-oriented concerns at each stage:

Stage	Concerns
Surviving	Loyalty or None
Connected	Merit and Rank
Confident	Heroism
Purposeful	Intrinsic
Transparent	Employee Experience
Intuitive	A Life Well Lived
Transcendent	Unnecessary; Abundance and gift economies

Beginning with the Surviving stage, the expectation from those considered to be 'strong' is that they receive unwavering loyalty from the 'weak'. The leaders take what they want and establish their higher rank through raw power, effectively rewarding and recognizing themselves in the process. The top ranks take their share before distributing any leftovers with others. In turn, those in the lower ranks expect to receive a share of the spoils of victory when displaying devotion and loyalty to the higher-ranking individuals. The other type of support behavior that can happen at this stage is that there simply is none. It is indeed 'every man for himself' and each individual is left to sink or swim on their own. If you unquestioningly continue to do what you are told then you might get to keep your job, your paycheck and whatever additional benefits may exist to support yourself. Nothing more is available to you unless you can take it for yourself.

Progressing into the Connected stage, expected behaviors are clearly defined through well documented roles, responsibilities, and processes. Conformity is expected, and the rigid hierarchy defines relative rank and authority. For those that display their merits by following the rules effectively and with the appropriate diplomacy, then they are rewarded and recognized accordingly, typically during some form of annual review process. By continuously performing well (i.e., either *meeting* or *exceeding* expectations) they may even be promoted in rank so that they receive the increased rewards and recognition associated with that next level in the hierarchy. The expectation is that by 'climbing the ladder' one is being both recognized and rewarded appropriately. The rewards at this stage are mostly provided through a structured system of base pay plus bonus that reflects one's rank in the organization.

The Confident level sets the stage for the emergence of the Hero. Those that go above and beyond the others, whether through superior knowledge and expertise or with an exertion of willpower that drives them to succeed and achieve, will be recognized and rewarded for their individual efforts. Putting in the extra hours, closing the big deal, and stepping up to meet project deadlines are the type of expected behaviors that generate the most benefits. With the profit-oriented nature of the Confident stage, rewards are exclusively material in nature coming in the form of pay, bonus, commissions, company shares and the like.

With the shift into the communal and empathetic Purposeful stage, recognizing individual achievers with material rewards is overtaken by the search for more intrinsic benefits that take all people into account. In addition to the other support structures that emerge at this stage, such as diversity and inclusion programs, actual rewards and recognition reflect that same support for employee wellbeing and engagement. Social recognition and intrinsic motivation take priority over financial considerations, both at the company and the individual level. Employee motivation and engagement become the objectives that are pursued through establishing appropriate environments and support structures. Included in that concept is paying people enough in salary to remove any possibility of money issues becoming a distraction to identifying and pursuing a meaningful purpose. Additional intrinsic motivation at the Purposeful stage comes from allowing people to work with autonomy and providing them the wherewithal to level up their chosen skills.

The Transparent stage takes intrinsic rewards to a whole new level. This is the level of immersive employee experiences where the intent is to make people feel good and live with purpose. Having a deep connection and a sense of purpose at work is a level of intrinsic reward that begins to blur the lines between 'work' and 'life'. Employees feel that the environment is supportive to the point where they can bring their whole authentic selves to work every day, and that self is recognized and valued by the organization. Transparency in pay begins to happen at this stage as companies publish compensation levels and continuously work to address any material pay discrepancies that may be identified. The capability to 'self-set' pay becomes a new way to provide monetary rewards in an openly communal fashion. Periodic performance reviews are eliminated as the basis for rewards and recognition moves toward continuous feedback, which is intended to facilitate the higher levels of satisfaction that come from being a part of entrepreneurial and self-organizing teams. Therefore, most recognition at this level is based on peer feedback and self-measuring if progress and results are being achieved. Previous individual rewards and recognition have shifted to being team-based, and results are made visible to everyone so that support can be provided and received through frequent feedback. As part of an immersive employee experience, solid feedback received through open and honest communications is deemed rewarding unto itself.

At the Intuitive stage, the main reward being sought after is a life well lived, as the evolving purpose of the organization aligns with what each individual believes they are called to do. Work no longer feels like work at this stage. Recognition and rewards come through openly celebrating rapid learning, doing what one believes is right, and experimenting and innovating without fear of so-called 'failure'. Material rewards, although still deemed necessary to some extent, are eliminated from being front of mind as the belief system has shifted from one of scarcity to one of abundance.

The Transcendent stage that follows virtually eliminates the concept of rewards and recognition altogether. At this stage, such rewards become unnecessary as the shift to a new worldview completely takes hold, one where the universe is known to be infinitely abundant and naturally takes care of all beings. In the resulting abundance economy, status and recognition are defined by one's reputation amongst peers for sharing what one has, not how much they keep for themselves.

Putting the Quadrant & Line Pieces Together

The descriptions of the various IMT stages of maturity show how these stages could be used to provide a general assessment of an organization, environment, team, or individual, e.g., a company operating at the Confident level or an individual operating at the Purposeful stage. To get a better idea of where a given entity is (or will be) with regards to Personal, Cultural, Employment, and Organizational characteristics, the same stage definitions can be leveraged to show the next level of detail by applying the stages to each IMT quadrant, as was seen in this diagram:

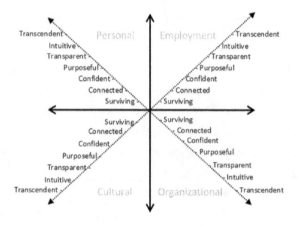

By expanding the IMT quadrant model yet again with the concept of Developmental Lines, there is now an additional level of detail that can be captured within each quadrant for a given entity. This results in the diagrammatic visualization below:

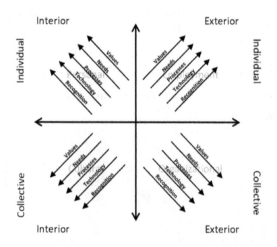

The level of complexity has just gone up significantly, as for any given entity we may have up to 25 different maturity assessments; 5 developmental line assessments for each of the quadrants (20 total), an average, generalization, or approximation of those lines for each quadrant (4) and an even higher-level average that describes all four quadrants together (1). Considering that there may be thousands of people working on hundreds of teams in multiple environments across the entire organization, that means there may be tens of thousands of pieces to the puzzle. A puzzle of this magnitude is substantially beyond the level of complexity that most people have ever tackled. The number of pieces and parts is inherently daunting and overwhelming. This is yet another insight as to why so many Modernization and Transformation initiatives continue to fail, as the natural human tendencies to reduce complexity and simplify approaches as much as possible means many of these pieces get left off of the table altogether. What is needed is a way to manage all of these pieces in a way that will connect them tightly with each other, bringing them together into a single cohesive picture.

Connecting the Pieces

At this point all we have done is dumped the entire set of puzzle pieces onto our table in a giant mixed up pile. The problem now is that this particular type of puzzle, piecing together a successful Modernization or Transformation program, is unlike one we've ever seen before. The pieces each have a unique appearance and the way they interconnect is completely different than a puzzle with which we are familiar. Before putting together an actual roadmap and plan for an IMT program, we need to learn the skills required to solve this type of problem effectively.

What has been defined so far are the types of pieces that the IMT model can use to represent both the current 'as-is' state and the desired 'to-be' future state. Both of these states can be captured for any organization, environmental component, team, or individual. The level of detail increases as we drill down through each diagram's quadrants and developmental lines. Given the sheer number of potential data points available, there is a need to capture and define these details in an efficient and effective manner. A manner that also provides a clear understanding at every level up and down the organization, from a single employee, through teams and environments, to the organization as a whole.

As Above So Below

The universe runs on natural laws, and throughout the history of civilization there has been a continuous pursuit of discovering these laws so that we might learn from them and put them to best use. The ancient philosophy of Hermeticism sought to capture these natural laws as seven principles that were enshrined in a work known as the Emerald Tablet, or *Tabula Smaragdina*. The second principle listed on the tablet, which has been used in many different contexts throughout the ages, is widely known to be "As Above, So Below"[26]. This is the Principle of Correspondence. The fully translated text is this:

> *'That which is above is like to that which is below, and that which is below is like to that which is above, to accomplish the miracles of one thing.'*[27]

The concept behind this principle is that hidden solutions to problems can be deduced by looking at what exists one layer above and one layer below the problem. This allows patterns to be inferred, as well as the nature of what lies in between. This principle is directly aligned with the concept of holons discussed earlier, as each layer being examined is a whole unit unto itself that is made up of parts from the layer below but is also a part of the layer above. By examining the characteristics of an organization, as well as the corresponding characteristics of the environments, teams, and individuals in that organization, the result is a better understanding of the true nature of the entity at all levels. This holds true whether we begin at the top of the chain, the bottom of the chain, or anywhere in between. The key to attaining this understanding is the process of *inference* that happens during the investigation. Patterns arise before completing an exhaustive investigation of every constituent component, e.g., scientists do not have to examine every single instance of a particular type of molecule to 'know' what atoms make up that molecule and how that molecule is incorporated in a certain single celled organism. The same holds true for assessing organizational layers during a Modernization or Transformation effort using IMT.

The key that unlocks this type of understanding is identifying a representative sample set. For a team of 10 people, it might seem fairly straight forward to do an IMT assessment on every individual as well as the team itself. This would provide 10 individual diagrams that describe all developmental lines for all quadrants, and a single team-level diagram that captures developmental lines for each of the Cultural, Employment and Organizational quadrants. The potential need for inference arises when completing the fourth aspect for the team diagram because the Personal quadrant will represent an *average approximation* of up to 10 different developmental line bar charts that individually capture what each team member thinks about the team itself. In this case, even if one or two of the team members are not included for whatever reason, the levels of maturity at the team stage can still be *inferred* from the other results. As certain aspects are targeted for improvements by a Modernization or Transformation effort, identifying which individuals, teams, and environments will be impacted determines what diagrams need to be generated as well as what constitutes a representative sample set for those entities.

To be able to uncover valid inferences, what is needed at this point is to identify the types of techniques that are effective methods for assessing the different types of entities. This will allow specific stages of maturity to be defined for all lines for all quadrants for all entities at all levels, or anything in between. The types of methods will differ depending on whether a specific assessment is gauging interior versus exterior aspects, as well as individual versus collective aspects. Below is a discussion of what types of techniques naturally align with each quadrant. It is then followed by details of how an IMT quadrant diagram is assembled for each type of entity by connecting the various quadrant assessments.

Personal Pieces

The Personal quadrant is the individual interior aspect that looks at the world through the eyes of a particular person. The Personal quadrant captures what individuals think about the entity in question; be it a team, an environment, the organization, or themselves. Therefore, when attempting to determine the stage of maturity for each of the 5 developmental lines in this quadrant, the assessment is completely focused on uncovering and understanding an individual's *thoughts, feelings, and beliefs* regarding the given entity. As none of these things can be 'seen' or 'touched' empirically, these assessments are typically completed by using techniques such as surveys, conversations, and observations. Regardless of the techniques being used, the assessment must be oriented around the fact that any investigative work is trying to uncover information on the 'individual interior'. Taking the survey technique as an example, the definitions of the developmental lines provided earlier can be used as something of an outline for the type of questions that might be asked. For example, when assessing the lines for the Personal quadrant of a particular individual, that person could be asked to respond to a survey that contains questions such as these:

- *Which of the following has the most influence on how you go about your work?*
    - ○ Staying employed
    - ○ My team's success and wellbeing
    - ○ Meeting company financial targets
    - ○ The wellbeing of all employees and customers
    - ○ Open and honest communication
    - ○ Being able to try new things without fear of failure
- *Which of the following is the most satisfying part of your job?*
    - ○ Getting paid
    - ○ Performing my duties well
    - ○ Personal achievement
    - ○ Working with a sense of purpose
    - ○ Working with autonomy
    - ○ Developing personal strengths and skills

In order to get a full set of responses that address all five developmental lines there may also be questions about how the survey participant would describe the processes that govern the work in their area, what they feel about the skills and technologies required to do their job, and how they ascertain or realize rewards and recognition for their work. Specific wording and responses would be determined by the actual context in which this person works, i.e., what their job is, what team(s) or group(s) they are a part of, and for which company they work. The answer options used as examples above are most likely too coarse and leading to realistically be used in practice, but they illustrate what such a survey would be attempting to uncover and understand. A better technique might be to allow for freeform text responses that allow the responder to provide true insight into their thinking. However, this may become less viable in situations where a significantly larger number of participants are needed to get a representative sample set regarding the non-individual entities of teams, environments and the entire organization. Either way, this example provides some directional guidance on how to go about using survey techniques as part of assessing the Personal (interior individual) quadrant in general.

As survey responses rarely provide enough information in and of themselves to perform a complete and accurate Personal assessment, having conversations directly with individuals will help to generate a more complete picture as to what stage of maturity each individual is working at across all 5 developmental lines. One of the most effective forms of conversational assessment techniques, which is a foundational piece of the Design Thinking process, is Empathy Interviews. As the Personal quadrant is the realm of the 'individual interior', one-on-one Empathy Interviews are appropriate because they are designed specifically to gain an understanding of the feelings and experiences of others, enabling the gathering of insights that might not be readily apparent. This is a human-centered technique that allows for a free-flowing conversation to naturally provide the necessary information to make an accurate assessment for each of the 5 development lines. By prefacing the conversation with a very rough agenda of the topics to be covered, topics that 'conveniently' correspond to the 5 lines, then the discussion can follow whatever tangents may arise. This technique has been proven to quickly get at what is most important and concerning to that person as you talk through what is working well and what is not. Using this technique to generate empathy with people is very often the quickest path to completing an assessment on the Personal quadrant for any entity.

Once the assessment information has been gathered, the corresponding stages of maturity can be plotted on a bar chart reflecting the current state of the Personal quadrant. The example below is a developmental lines bar chart capturing a particular individual's thoughts about themselves:

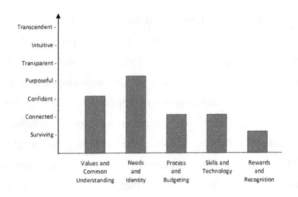

An average approximation of maturity across this person's developmental lines can then be plotted on the IMT quadrant chart being built for this individual:

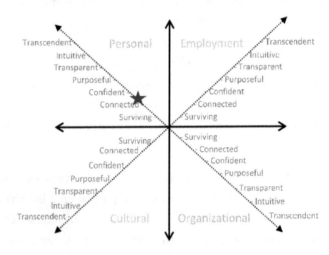

For any other entity being assessed that is related to multiple individuals such as a team, environmental component, or the organization itself, the gauging of the maturity level in the

Personal quadrant is done by averaging or approximating the Personal quadrant assessments of a representative sample of individual constituent team members. The types of questions asked, or topics discussed, can also be narrowed down to include only those that are directly relevant to the entity being assessed, such as what they think about a particular budgeting process, how well they think a certain technology is working, or how the company's annual review process makes them feel. Again, when completing the Personal quadrant, it represents what people *think, feel,* and *believe* about a particular entity, so the questions and discussions should be framed appropriately to obtain the relevant information and insights. To summarize, the table below shows the specific concerns of the Personal quadrant based on the type of entity being assessed:

Entity	Personal Quadrant Concerns
Individual	What the person thinks about themselves*
Team	Average approximation of what individuals think about the team
Environment	What an individual thinks about something in their personal environment, or an average approximation of what individuals think about a shared environmental entity
Organization	The average approximation of what all individuals think about the company as a whole

* When completing an Individual IMT diagram there is the potential to capture what other individuals think about this individual, but this is not recommended unless the organization is operating at least at the Transparent stage when peer reviews are standard practice along with advice and conflict resolution processes.

Cultural Pieces

The Cultural quadrant is the collective interior aspect that views the relevant part of the organization being assessed through the lens of a team or group. Therefore, this is the quadrant that gauges the collective thinking for any given set of individuals, whether that be a team, team of teams, department or other organizational function. In the same fashion as the Personal quadrant, the stage of maturity for the developmental lines in this quadrant is based on the *thoughts, feelings, and beliefs* that exist regarding the entity being assessed. The difference between the Cultural and Personal quadrants is that in the Cultural quadrant, the developmental lines reflect the *common* beliefs regarding the entity in question, so even though a particular individual may think differently, this does not necessarily represent what the entire group thinks as a singular entity.

Many of the methods that can be used for assessments in this quadrant are the same as the Personal quadrant, such as surveys, conversations, and observations. What changes is that the questions and discussion points in the Cultural quadrant shift to consider the teams' point of view rather than that of a single individual. For example, when assessing the Cultural quadrant for a particular team by using a survey, the framing of the investigation might move to something like this:

- *Which of the following has the most impact on the work performed by your team?*
    - o Individual team member concerns

- o   Team cohesion
- o   Company financial targets
- o   Company purpose and values
- o   Transparent communications
- o   Safe to experiment and fail

- • *Which of the following has recently provided significant benefit to your team?*
  - o   Continued employment
  - o   Clearly defined roles and responsibilities
  - o   Completing projects on-time and under-budget
  - o   Meeting specific customer needs
  - o   Being allowed to self-manage and self-organize
  - o   Being given opportunities to develop and grow skills and expertise

In the same fashion as the Personal quadrant assessment, by asking similar team-oriented questions for the remaining developmental lines, the team's Cultural quadrant results are focused on what this team collectively thinks, feels, and believes about the team itself. Going beyond the one-on-one orientation of the Personal quadrant, doing a form of Empathy Interview with the entire team assembled together can be one of the most effective methods for determining a collective set of thoughts, feelings, and beliefs, as each individual will be influenced and 'play off of' each other during the conversation.

The use of a Niko-Niko Calendar, or 'mood board' is another effective technique for assessing how a team is feeling. This practice provides a somewhat objective measure for team motivation and well-being. As the goal is to gauge an overall sense of how the team is feeling, the measurement does not have to be highly precise because it will still generate clues for further investigation as to what is causing the emotions and moods recorded on the board. Below is an example of a Niko-Niko Calendar:

Sprint 33	Mon	Tue	Wed	Thur	Fri	Mon	Tue	Wed	Thur	Fri
Lucinda	😃	😊	😊	😐	😐	😊	😊	😐	😊	😊
Theodore	😡	😊	😠	😠	😠	😊	😊	😊	😡	😊
Virginia	😐	😐	😐	😐	😡	😊	😐	😊	😊	😊
Olga	😊	😊	😊	😐	😐	😊	😀	😐	😊	😐
Elliot	😃	😊	😊	😐	😐	😊	😡	😊	😊	😊
Suresh	😐	😊	😊	😐	😐	😊	😊	😐	😊	😊
Emile	😊	😞	😊	😐	😐	😊	😡	😊	😐	😊

[28]

Assessing the relative maturity level of an entity's Cultural component is plotted using IMT bar charts and quadrant diagrams in the same manner as when assessing the Personal quadrant. Using an example of capturing a team's assessment of itself, plotting the average approximation of the developmental lines in the Cultural quadrant might look like the following:

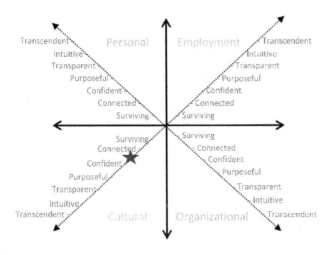

Being the 'collective interior' aspect, the Cultural quadrant may have to capture the perspective of several different teams in order to provide a more well-rounded assessment. If the entity being assessed is indeed a particular team, then the Cultural quadrant of the IMT diagram captures what that team thinks, feels, and believes about itself, but it can also capture what *other* teams think about that team. The Cultural quadrant for an individual IMT diagram may need to represent what various teams think about that individual, not just the first level team of which the person is a member. An Employment or Organization diagram's Cultural quadrant could provide differing viewpoints regarding what several teams think about a particular policy, process, tool, technology, physical environment, or the organization itself. That all said, below is a summarization of the Cultural quadrant viewpoint that is captured for each type of entity:

Entity	Cultural Quadrant Concerns
Individual	What the team(s) think about this individual (possible drill-down scenario)
Team	What the team(s) think about this team (possible drill-down scenario)
Environment	What the team(s) think about this environmental entity (possible drill-down scenario)
Organization	Average approximation of what all teams think about the organization as a whole

The fact that this quadrant may need to capture varying viewpoints of multiple teams to complete a full assessment creates a different level of depth and complexity that can be addressed through the use of multiple nested IMT diagrams. This requires a method to address the 'drill-down' scenarios noted in the table above.

Recalling the discussion on holons, a Cultural quadrant assessment may require the collection and differentiation of what different teams think about the entity in question. For example, a Product team may believe that an IT delivery team is 'slow and expensive' while that IT delivery team thinks very differently about itself. This creates a specific 'drill-down' scenario where multiple IMT bar charts and their average approximations become embedded within the Cultural quadrant for this particular team. Using this type of layered approach allows an assessment to capture an average approximation across all teams (which would look the same as the Cultural quadrant IMT diagram above) as well as the capability to see at a more granular level what different sub-groups think, feel, and believe about the team in question. This is visualized in the nested IMT diagram below:

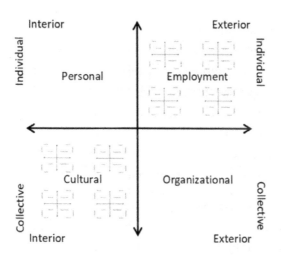

Employment Pieces

The Employment quadrant is the individual exterior aspect that captures the assessment of a particular component in the environment. Moving to the right-hand 'exterior' side of the IMT diagram, we are now in the realm of the tangible and empirical. A work environment is made up of the physical elements that can affect when, where and how people work. Performing an assessment of the Employment quadrant is inherently more structured and straight forward than trying to 'extract' the unseen thoughts, feelings, and beliefs relative to the 'interior' half of the diagram. Assessing some portion of the environment that people are employing for specific purposes is where an extensive amount of content and structured approaches have existed for many years. These types of efforts typically include reviews of various processes, tools, technologies, physical environments, and other related artifacts such as reports, documents, or working software. The activities performed for information gathering in these areas are what most people are familiar with when it comes to assessing organizations, their capabilities, and their processes. Documentation is gathered and reviewed, observations are made while activities are in progress, and gaps, opportunities, and recommendations are generated accordingly.

There are several well-known models that have been built to assess process maturity, such as the Capability Maturity Models (CMM/CMMi), International Organization for Standardization (ISO), Information Technology Information Library (ITIL), Control Objectives for IT (COBIT), and Lean Six Sigma. There are also several models that go beyond various business processes to explicitly include technology solutions as part of the 'Enterprise Architecture', such as the Zachman Framework and The Open Group Architectural Forum (TOGAF). In most cases a given company will have already invested time and effort in this space that can be leveraged for an IMT assessment, but if not, then any of the models listed here can help frame an investigation into what currently exists relative to the intent and objectives of the Modernization or Transformation initiative.

When assessing all 5 developmental lines in the Employment quadrant, the relative maturity level of the Processes & Budgeting, Skills & Technology, and Rewards & Recognition lines will be objectively observable in how they relate to one another, although one particular line will typically be the most aligned with the entity being assessed. For example, a budgetary approval process that requires extensive up-front project scope definition and estimations of project costs and timelines will be directly aligned with Processes & Budgeting line. There will be related impacts on the Skills & Technologies needed to support and execute the process as it is defined, and the results of meeting the parameters set out in that process may also be reflected in how Rewards & Recognition are handed out. When doing an IMT assessment of this particular budgeting approach, the process itself will also reflect certain values and perceived needs that can be captured in the other 2 developmental lines. An example diagram showing the average approximation of the development lines for the budget process described above may look something like this:

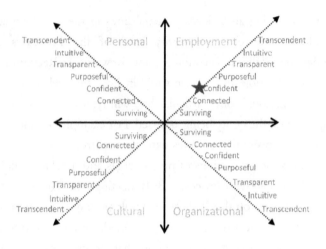

The Employment quadrant is also similar to the Cultural quadrant in that a nested set of IMT diagrams may be necessary to generate a multi-faceted assessment. When generating an individual IMT diagram, the Employment quadrant might represent that person's complete working environment, but for the purposes of the IMT initiative, there may be a need to break that down into component pieces that are assessed independently. The same would hold true when assessing a team environment. The Employment quadrant, when assessing an environment component itself, would reflect an objective assessment of the entity from a maturity perspective, or an average approximation across its component parts. For the overall organization IMT diagram, this quadrant would represent a maturity assessment that summarizes all environmental considerations as one with the potential to drill-down into any constituent component. These Employment quadrant assessment viewpoints are summarized below:

Entity	Employment Quadrant Concerns
Individual	The personal work environment relative to this individual (possible drill-down scenario)
Team	The shared work environment for this team (possible drill-down scenario)
Environment	Objective maturity assessment of the work environment component itself (possible drill-down scenario)
Organization	Average approximation of all company-wide environments (possible drill-down scenario)

Organizational Pieces

The Organizational quadrant is the collective exterior aspect that represents the maturity assessment of the shared environments across the entire company. Still being on the right-hand side of the IMT model, this quadrant is assessed through empirical evidence gathered by utilizing many of the same tools and techniques used for the Employment quadrant. When assessing the entire organization, this quadrant will reflect the level of maturity across all common company-wide policies, processes, tools, technologies, physical environments, and other related artifacts and documentation. Therefore, the maturity assessments at that level will review things like the complete Enterprise Architecture, financial and budgeting processes, organization structures, product and service offerings, and company values, mission and strategy. In addition to the models and techniques listed above for the Employment quadrant, there are also more comprehensive organizational change frameworks, such as the Burke-Litwin Model[29], and complete business and technical assessment models such as the Enterprise Architecture Assessment Framework (EAAF)[30] published by the United States Government. These types of models and frameworks can be helpful starting points if sufficient materials do not already exist at the company being assessed.

An organizational assessment will typically be aligned with a particular stage of maturity based on the stage descriptions provided in the Big Pieces - Stages of Maturity section above. For example, an organization that is predominantly driven by quarterly financial shareholder reports, funds its projects based on business cases built on detailed estimates of cost, time, and scope, and pays out employee bonuses based on attaining EBITDA targets, the associated organizational quadrant might look something like this:

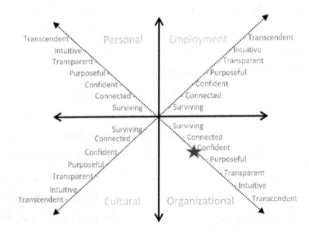

When assessing any sub-entity of the organization, the IMT diagram's Organizational quadrant will reflect how organization-wide tools, technologies, policies, and procedures influence and relate to the entity in question. So, based on our last example, if a particular individual is paid a bonus based on company EBITDA and other company policies that apply to them also reflect the drive for profitability, achievement, and expertise, then the organizational quadrant would look exactly like the one above. Given the inherent company-wide nature of the 'collective exterior' content described by this aspect, it will be very common for the organizational quadrant to be relatively stable across all entities at all levels. The specific viewpoint reflected in the Organizational quadrant for each type of entity is listed below:

Entity	Organizational Quadrant Concerns
Individual	Company-wide environmental components that apply to or directly influence this individual (possible drill-down scenario)
Team	Company-wide environmental components that apply to or directly influence this team (possible drill-down scenario)
Environment	Company-wide environmental components that apply or directly influence this environmental component (possible drill-down scenario)
Organization	Average approximation of all company-wide environments

There is a very subtle nuance to this quadrant relative to the Employment quadrant when building an IMT diagram for an individual, team, or environment. While the Employment quadrant will reflect what is actually *in use* by that entity, the Organizational quadrant will reflect broader environmental components that are *relevant* to that entity in that they may periodically apply or directly influence the entity. For example, a software development team may be using AngularJS to build web applications, which could be part of the Employment quadrant assessment for the team or the environment (or both). The Organizational quadrant for both of them would gauge the enterprise architecture and organizational strategy that dictate *why* web applications are being built at all.

It is also worth noting that as we approach the single IMT diagram that represents the entire organization, the contents of the Employment and Organizational quadrants will converge. As both reflect the sum of all environments, any 'drill-down' content in the Employment quadrant can be used here while the Organizational quadrant can take the role of the average approximation of maturity across the entire company. This now leads us to define exactly how these quadrants connect with each other for each type of entity.

Individual Connections

After leveraging the developmental lines to assess each IMT quadrant, a complete IMT diagram can be compiled for a particular entity that fully reflects its four-fold nature. When completing an IMT quadrant chart for a single person, the Personal quadrant will reflect what that person believes about themselves, and potentially what other individuals think about the individual in question. The other 3 quadrants (Cultural, Employment, and Organizational) will all be assessed through a filter that considers only the pieces of those quadrants that are directly relevant to that person, such as how the team(s) view that person, what this person's individual environment consists of (processes, technologies, rewards, physical environment, etc.), and which organization-wide environmental components apply or have direct influence on them.

Perhaps an assessment has been completed for an individual that identified their thoughts, feelings, and beliefs about themselves are at the low end of the Connected stage of maturity, while, at the same time, their team views them as operating in more of an individualistic and ad-hoc fashion characteristic of the Surviving level. This person's work environment is somewhat advanced technologically but lagging a bit behind in terms of process and recognition maturity, resulting in an overall Employment assessment of low-to-mid-range Confident. The organization overall is fully operating at the Confident level, which is where the same process and rewards characteristics seen in the Employment quadrant for this individual are the same across the company and most activities are oriented around profit and shareholder value. Therefore, this individual's current state IMT diagram looks something like this:

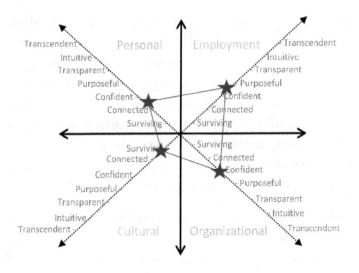

A quick glance at this individual's IMT diagram provides a clue that there may be something worth investigating in the team dynamic surrounding this person. Completing other individual IMT diagrams for team members and a diagram for the team itself will help determine if any associated actions should be directed toward the team as a whole or just with certain individuals. Either way, a potential for growth and maturity will be uncovered that can be directly addressed if necessary.

The Individual IMT diagram has the potential to be expanded with additional 'drill-down' content in any or all of the Personal, Cultural, and Employment quadrants if it is relevant to the direction and intent of the IMT program itself.

Team Connections

Compiling an IMT chart for a particular team will reflect an average approximation of what various individuals think about the team in question (Personal), what that team's environment consists of (Employment), and what company-wide environmental components affect this team (Organizational). The Cultural quadrant will express or articulate what this team thinks about itself, and if necessary, will also expand (in a nested fashion) to include what other teams think about this team. The Employment quadrant may also leverage the nesting approach to break down the team environment into its component parts.

As an example of a team IMT diagram, let's say a Customer and User Experience team (CX/UX) believes themselves to be very much oriented in creating the best customer journey possible through the company's products, and each individual team member is also operating and engaging with that same intent. Their environment contains all the most recent tools and technologies used to do journey mapping, perform user interface modeling, create stunning designs, and work with a Lean Startup 'build-measure-learn' cycle. The organization still requires them to be funded as part of an associated software development project that is targeted to deliver a new product release in six months. This causes friction with who the team believes they are and how they should operate. This belief conflicts with the constraints put on them by the current company processes and structures. Therefore, the team, and the average of its members, are both operating at the Purposeful stage and pushing toward Transparent, and some of their environment is reflecting this, but the company itself is deeply rooted at the Confident stage. The result, and the described friction, is seen in the maturity plotting on the team's IMT diagram below:

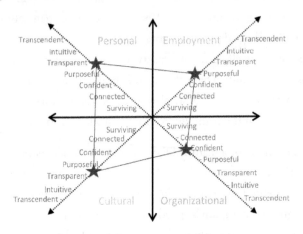

Similar to Individual IMT diagrams, a Team IMT diagram has the potential to be expanded with additional 'drill-down' content in any or all of the Personal, Cultural, and Employment quadrants. In the case of this example, a 'drill-down' in the Employment quadrant would show a higher-level maturity in the processes, tools, and techniques being specifically applied to the customer-centric and Lean Startup activities (Purposeful and/or Transparent), while other processes and budget concerns would reflect the more Confident nature of the broader organization.

Environmental Connections

An Environmental IMT diagram is used to capture the assessment for any policy, process, tool, technology, or physical environment. Compiling an IMT chart for a particular environmental component will reflect an average approximation of what various individuals think about the component in question (Personal), what teams think about that part of the environment (Cultural), and which company-wide environmental components have an influence on this entity. The Employment quadrant will reflect an objective empirical assessment of the entity across the 5 developmental lines.

An environmental IMT diagram has the most potential for complexity with regards to the possibility of having multiple layers of granularity in any, or all of the four quadrants. As much of what occurs in a Modernization or Transformation initiative is focused on directly changing process and technology, environmental IMT diagrams will be leveraged extensively to determine incremental steps to effectively attain higher levels of maturity.

To illustrate the depth of nesting in the environment, consider that a single IDT (integrated development environment) is composed of multiple tools but also has a relationship to a shared development environment, which may in turn relate to various types of integrated and operational environments. The chain will eventually lead all the way up to a representation of the full Enterprise Architecture in use across the organization.

Each layer is an individual item that can be 'employed' by itself but is also an integral part of some larger entity. This provides a full range of depth that can be leveraged to whatever level is appropriate based on the goals and objectives of the assessment as well as the Modernization or Transformation initiative itself.

For a diagrammatic example, a cloud-based microservices application that has been developed reflects a Transparent level of maturity, while the team that built it strictly complied with the provided microservices architecture, with each and every team member believing that it details the *only* way to build applications correctly. This is all occurring in an organization that provides third party services to its clients who contracted this team to deliver a specific final product (scope) in a fixed timeframe for a fixed cost. The IMT result for the application itself, being a specific part of the overall environment being assessed, would be the following:

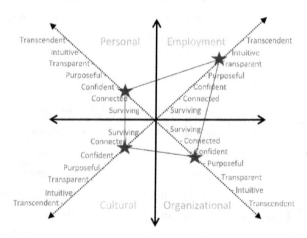

The lack of balance across the four quadrants in this IMT diagram helps identify multiple risks that can be addressed as part of the IMT program. Even though technologically there is a high level of maturity, without bringing the employees, teams, and organization up to the corresponding level, there are inherent risks around being able to gracefully handle the 'unknown unknowns' that will emerge during a software development effort. Quality will suffer, individual microservices may not be as fully transparent and as flexible as necessary, and 'non-compliant' team members may become flight risks to the organization.

The Organization Connection

Every organization will have one, and only one, quadrant diagram that represents the summation and average maturity of all people, groups, environments and organizational structures (all quadrants) across the entire company. This is the 'source' diagram that acts as the container for all lower level holons. The viewpoint reflected at this level on the left-hand side is what all individuals and teams think about the company, while the right represents the maturity level of all processes and technologies. The organization IMT diagram is a snapshot of the company at a point in time, which could be the current state or the intended future state. The number of pieces that make up this picture will be determined by the size and type of the organization itself. The subset of those pieces that need to be assessed and matured will be driven by the goals, objectives, and intended outcomes of the

Modernization or Transformation initiative relative to the current state.

This becomes a point of interest at this level because, as was seen in the other types of IMT diagrams, an imbalance across the quadrants will highlight certain types of issues and risks that need to be addressed simply to achieve some type of balance. At the organizational level, balance across the quadrants may be exactly why a Modernization or Transformation initiative is needed. The organization itself sits within a broader context of ever-changing market dynamics, customer demands, and competitor disruptions. A company that has been successful for several decades operating at the Connected or Confident stage might very well become the sterotypical 'dinosaur' that, by not evolving, will simply age and fade away while the rest of the world moves onward and upward. These types of companies frequently have aging technologies and workforces as new entrants in both areas naturally gravitate to other organizations where they can grow and thrive. The following diagram, as an example, depicts a well-balanced organization, but it could very well represent an existential threat and a need to adapt or die:

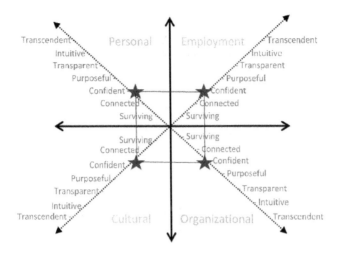

If we were to superimpose the organizational diagram of a competitor to this company that is working at the Purposeful stage, it would completely envelop this organization, as if they are being totally surrounded and consumed. That simple visualization may be saying a lot about how much work and effort must be undertaken in order to ensure the company's continued survival. Now is the time to take all of these pieces and start using them to solve the puzzle.

Solving the Puzzle

Now that we have learned the types of puzzle pieces that exist and how they interconnect, we can start to apply that knowledge to the task at hand. It is time to lay out a specific strategy, plan, and framework for an Integral Modernization or Transformation (IMT) initiative. When sitting down to piece together a jigsaw puzzle of the 'big picture', many people will begin with sorting pieces by color and pattern, effectively breaking it down into manageable subtasks before the work of connecting the pieces actually begins. Setting up an IMT program is very similar in that there needs to be an initial function created to identify what subtasks will be required to meet the company's Modernization and Transformation objectives. But before those subtasks can even be identified, the first step that is needed is to assemble the right team that will be capable of establishing and driving the IMT program itself.

Assemble the Dissectologists

It is not a word that is used all that often, but the term 'dissectologist' refers to someone who enjoys, and experiences benefits from doing jigsaw puzzles. The name comes from the fact that the first puzzles were maps pasted on wood and cut (dissected) into small pieces that could be pieced back together. For any Modernization or Transformation program there will be some group that has ultimate responsibility for planning, oversight and reporting on progress, and if the IMT approach is going to be successful, then this group needs to have a bit of that dissectologist nature in them. They will have to be able to identify the multitude of component pieces, relate them to each other, and be able to connect them into an achievable vision for the program. That said, this is no longer simplistically comparable to the leisurely assembly of a jigsaw puzzle. There will most likely be millions of dollars put into the effort and the company could very well be staking its future on becoming something new and substantially different from what it is today. This is no game. It is about evolutionary survival and the team responsible for managing it needs to be able to shoulder that burden, as well as the multidimensional responsibilities that come with it.

Many organizations will assign the role of program delivery to something like a Project Portfolio Management (PPM) team or Enterprise Program Management Office (EPMO), while others may set up a 'Transformation Office' (TO) or 'Transformation Management Office' (TMO). Transformation Offices are usually different from established project and program management functions in that a TO is generally a temporary governance and delivery vehicle whose singular purpose is to oversee and drive the successful implementation of critical programs or projects that enable organizational transformation. Going forward, the term Transformation Office (TO) will be used to represent any such organizational structure that is managing and overseeing the day-to-day work that happens within a Modernization or Transformation effort.

Regardless of the chosen team's name, it is imperative that the group responsible for managing the program has direct accountability to the C-suite. With the amount of investment involved as well as the potential impact on the company's going concern, this is not a responsibility that can be wholly delegated to the TO or a particular executive. The TO represents both the holistic vantage point and the daily vigilance that the program demands but, knowing that the use of the IMT model may highlight work to be done in *any* part of the company, continuous collaboration with the entire group of top executives will be necessary. Capturing the 'to-be' vision and using IMT to identify the impacted entities will lead to working with members of the executives' respective teams on the details of particular assessments and improvements. This requires that the executives help to clear a path for their teams, providing the needed bandwidth and support that allows them to participate and fully engage with the program. This is best accomplished by helping the teams prioritize their work in an explicit fashion with an understanding that this is not 'add on' or 'side of the desk' work on top of what are already full plates. The executive team will also be needed to provide guidance and course corrections based on incremental progress and results, as well as any external factors that may have emerged, so the program can keep driving toward the desired outcomes. Therefore, the assembly of the Transformation Office team must address multiple critical needs. The TO team must have the cross-functional skills needed to be able to manage the details of the program using the IMT model, be capable of collaborating with any number and type of other internal teams, and also be able to effectively work with the C-suite in both a reporting and advisory capacity. No small task, but this is no small effort and building the right team begins to reduce program risk right from the start. Once this team has been assembled and put in place, their purpose and directive can be shared with everyone in the company so that expectations are made clear. By communicating the Transformation Office's reason-for-being across the entire organization, it begins to establish an environment of transparency that will be critical to the success of the program going forward.

Transparency is especially critical for any Modernization or Transformation initiative, and therefore must be front of mind, not only when running the program, but even more so when staffing the Transformation Office. Most of the approach and techniques that will be recommended below are rooted in what was seen in the descriptions of the Transparent and Intuitive stages of maturity. Therefore, most, if not all of the members of the TO team should be operating at or at least near those levels. This may present a bit of a conundrum when the organization in question is not yet approaching those stages. The underlying risk when assembling the team is that the TO becomes staffed with people who have the knowledge of the processes, tools, and techniques needed to do the job, but their capability to execute effectively is inherently limited due to their actual maturity level. This typically results in much *'doing'* of tasks, but very little *'being'* in the appropriate mindset on a day-to-day basis. This problem manifests itself when the performing of these tasks is approached and executed with behaviors characteristic of other stages. For example, consider an individual who is certified in some form of Agile process who demands others observe strict compliance to the process as written and blindly adhere to 'increment' plans the teams 'committed' to, even in the light of conflicting evidence. This person's approach is actually inhibiting the potential benefits of adaptability and flexibility that are the intended outcomes of becoming Agile in the first place. This is someone who may *believe* themselves to be operating at a Transparent or Intuitive level because of their learned process knowledge, but they are actually operating somewhere around the Connected and Confident stages. Being able to identify and sense these types of conflicts between qualifications, beliefs, and behaviors becomes critical to building a TO team that can effectively fulfill its purpose.

Building a balanced Transformation Office also entails a 'right-sizing' of the team so they can fulfill their purpose but not become bloated or diluted in ways that go beyond that purpose. Reiterating the purpose of a TO from above, their *'singular purpose is to oversee and drive the successful implementation of critical programs or projects that enable organizational transformation'*. Therefore, when determining who will be 'doing' any of the change initiatives identified through the IMT assessments and modeling, the TO team should not be staffed or augmented with any skills that would be redundant to other functions that exist in the organization. The goal is to leverage what others in the company are already doing. For example, if there is a Corporate Communications function, then that group should be the company's source of information for who the TO is, why they exist, what they've accomplished, and what to expect from them going forward. This will also apply when working with specific IMT entities across the organization, such as the Enterprise Architecture or various processes and documentation, which we'll discuss in more detail momentarily. After the Transformation Office has been established, the Modernization or Transformation effort can begin in earnest. As was mentioned in Choosing the Right Puzzle, the TO can now drive the creation of the detailed image of the company's 'to-be' vision of the future.

Custom-Made Puzzles

No two companies are exactly alike. Therefore, no two IMT programs will be striving for the exact same future state. Each organization needs to paint its own picture of who they wish to become. Buying a puzzle off the shelf that has someone else's picture is not what is needed here, because setting out to copy someone else's success doesn't work for Modernization or Transformation. Many companies have fallen for consulting company's 'bulletproof plans' or 'recipes' for Digital Transformation that sell a one-size-fits-all approach. The 75% failure rate shows this to be patently false and that a context-specific approach needs to be identified. What is needed is the creation of a custom-made puzzle that is meaningful to this particular company and its people.

The first bits of information the Transformation Office requires in order to paint this custom picture are the top-level outcomes, objectives and goals that the IMT program is intended to achieve. There may be specific problems that need to be solved, changing customer and market needs, or certain opportunities that might be seized upon, all of which define an impetus for spinning up the program itself. To know where this program is headed, the TO needs to collaborate with the C-suite executives, perhaps in some sort of a facilitated workshop format, to generate a detailed picture of what the company is setting out to accomplish and why. The results of this can be captured in summary as a hypothesis that becomes the touchstone for the entire IMT program. *'If we do these things, we expect to solve X, enable Y, and become something new that looks like this'.* The *'looks like this'* portion of that hypothesis will address the reasons that led to the Modernization or Transformation, which are typically one or more of the contributing factors discussed in A Picture That Catches the Eye above. The level of detail that is added to this type of visionary hypothesis defines what a 'quality' outcome will look like in the future state. Every effort within the IMT program will be directly aligned with moving closer to this vision, and therefore everyone in the company will also need to be made aware of the impending journey.

From the outset, it is important to supply a narrative around the program to create conviction around the change. In many failed initiatives there has been no buy-in and no desire to expend the extra energy. The executive team doesn't directly address the skills in the organization and key people don't get freed up from their day jobs. Communicating clearly the captured vision and purpose of the IMT program and setting expectations for how various teams will be engaged, creates an image that everyone can begin to visualize and rally around.

Set Up the Workspace

In any company at any moment there will always be more work to do than can be staffed and funded at any given time. The unavoidable reality of capacity and budget constraints needs to be directly addressed as part of the IMT effort and continuously managed by the TO. Assuming that the environment is one where funding is being allocated to the Modernization or Transformation effort (and not one where 'cost is no object'), decisions need to be made with regards to what is the most valuable thing to work on with the currently available funding and capacity. Enter the concepts of Lean Portfolio Management (LPM)[31] and Beyond Budgeting[32], both of which apply lean principles to connect strategy to execution while enabling organizational adaptability and nimbleness. These principles are normally put into practice through the use of a Kanban system[33] that in effect defines the size of the available workspace where the next section of the puzzle can be pulled in, pieced together and completed.

Lean Portfolio Management handles work efforts in a distinctly different way from a typical annual budgeting process. Let's say a company has $60 Million allocated to their Transformation effort for the year. Many organizations will default to a pattern of allocating all $60 Million across multiple efforts or 'projects' at the first of the year and start them all concurrently. The problem that arises when taking this approach is that it is not actually known if all of those efforts are going to be the *right* things to be working on for an *entire* year. This puts the program at risk before anything even gets started. Taking a different view by using the principles of LPM and Beyond Budgeting, a form of business agility can be enabled that allows program risk to be mitigated continuously. If we consider the available funding as a burn rate of $5 Million per month instead of $60 Million per year, we could start with a discussion of what are the top priority efforts to spend that first $5 Million on. Toward the end of that first month we can discuss, for any of the efforts that haven't been completed, if they should continue, be adjusted, or be stopped because results are lacking, or priorities and circumstances have changed. The results of that discussion will determine the amount of funding available for the upcoming month to either allocate to in-flight efforts (adjusting each of them up or down as appropriate) or to launch new efforts. The overall burn rate of $5 Million per month is also up for discussion and can be raised or lowered accordingly based on the guidance of the C-suite. The amount of flexibility this provides enables the IMT program to continually adjust the plans based on the results observed. By evaluating progress and adjusting the plans as necessary on a recurring basis, the LPM approach provides a heartbeat-like rhythm that drives and paces the Modernization or Transformation effort. To put this function into practice, there needs to be a list of potential efforts generated that the executive team reviews and determines those that can be put in motion.

Turn Over the Pieces

Once the image of the future state has been captured, the question becomes '*how do we get there from here?*'. That question begs two other questions – '*where is* **here**?' and '*how will we know when we get* **there**?'. This is the time for leveraging the IMT techniques to capture the 'as-is' and 'to-be' states of the organization and the parts of the company that will be impacted by the Modernization or Transformation effort. The 'as-is' current state diagrams will define the 'here', the 'to-be' future state defines the 'there', and the gaps in between will reveal what steps need to be taken between the two states of being.

The members of the Transformation Office can capture diagrams for the current and future states concurrently if there is capacity on the team to do so. In order to create a useful comparison between the two states, it will be necessary to identify the sources of information that will be required to create the IMT diagrams, using the IMT program hypothesis for guidance and scope control. At a minimum there will need to be top-level Organization 'as-is' and 'to-be' diagrams created, and the relevant 'drill-down' content in the Cultural and

Employment quadrants will need to be identified, assessed, and associated diagrams created. Part of the planning for this assessment phase will be to identify the size of the sample sets required to capture an average approximation for all development lines in all quadrants of the Organization diagram. This may very well include individuals and teams that are not intended to be directly impacted by the IMT program itself but are necessary to understand and capture the true Personal and Cultural aspects that exist within the company. This is an important step because achieving a balanced future state will likely require some influencing and maturation across all people and teams.

With the potential for large amounts of information to be gathered, and many IMT diagrams generated that need to be tied together, there will need to be a workspace created and maintained by the TO team. Luckily there have been significant advances in online collaboration tools, such as Miro and Mural[34], that provide an unlimited canvas with the capability to embed multiple workspaces, custom chart and grid templates, and access controls to subsections of the overall diagram. These are great tools for the nested nature of the IMT diagrams and associated bar charts for developmental lines. What this also enables is visibility of the work in progress and the status of the IMT program overall. With the TO team being built around Transparent and Intuitive principles, having a tool such as this allows the IMT program to lead by example in terms of transparency and agility. It can control and limit when necessary depending on the overall maturity of the company itself.

While performing the capture of the current state, the TO team will need to work with groups across the entire organization. There will be interviews to be performed, surveys created and distributed, work observations, documentation reviews, and any other types of techniques required to make a solid and valuable set of IMT diagrams. As mentioned above, the Transformation Office is a collaborative function that should work with existing groups to execute this assessment. There will most likely be work with numerous and varied teams to complete assessments across all functions including technology, product, customer experience (CX), finance, risk, people (HR), operations, strategy, PMO, leadership, and sales and marketing. Modernization and Transformation are holistic concerns, and the initial assessment is the first activity that broadcasts to the entire organization that they are all in this together. It is through this breadth of analysis that the initial opportunities and potential efforts are identified as those that will truly get at the root of what is keeping the organization at its current level of maturity in multiple areas. The gaps between the current and future states will become clear as the IMT modeling progresses, but there is something even more valuable to the initiative that gets brought to light as well. Multiple strengths will be identified across the various organizational entities, as well as 'shadows' that signal a lack of readiness for the next stage of maturation. Many Modernization and Transformation efforts have failed simply by not acknowledging their strengths and weaknesses across all four IMT quadrants. Explicit identification and understanding of strengths and shadows will influence how the IMT roadmap is built and how progress toward the vision will be achieved.

Provide Strong Lights

As companies progress from the Connected stage to the Confident stage, space is made for people to pursue individual achievement and increase expertise in their chosen fields. Embedded in this phase of evolution is a shift from conforming to explicit roles and expectations, to one of finding what people are naturally good at and which ones have an interest in further developing those skills. For any company that is currently in the Confident stage, or has passed through it, an IMT assessment will highlight many folks throughout the company that have clear and valuable strengths. These strengths are not just valuable to the company, they are potential champions and leaders for the Modernization or Transformation effort itself. They can be additional lights that guide the way.

As was called out in the movement to the Purposeful stage of maturity, there is a shift from a deficit to a strength-based paradigm that occurs. For individuals that have made a conscious effort to gain knowledge and expertise in their own areas, they have established an attitude of learning and growth that can be leveraged across the entire program. There will be pilot programs and experimental initiatives that are geared toward proving that a particular approach to maturation is effective in the current environment. By identifying and noting particular strengths across the organization, when launching those efforts, they can include many of those same individuals. Allowing them to play to their strengths, leveraging their drive to learn and grow, and knowing that they are part of a larger purpose drives increased engagement and enthusiasm.

For initiatives where specific knowledge and skills do not yet exist as in-house strengths, being cognizant of the pitfalls of taking a 'buy' versus 'build' approach to retooling and upskilling will allow for better alignment with the long-term program objectives. When establishing new skills and behaviors, guidance and coaching can be provided with short-term external help while building internal strengths over the long-term. Leaving the work to a temporary team of 'experts' often results in a lack of skills and ongoing support of the initiative by those who remain. With so many Modernization and Transformation initiatives failing, increasing the number of champions and supporters across the organization is critical to establishing positive momentum for the program. As any sports fan knows, a shift in momentum and belief can be the difference between winning and losing. Putting the right people in the right environment where they can play to their strengths will not only contribute to the success of incremental efforts, it will start a momentum shift that influences others who might still have limiting beliefs which keep them 'stuck' in their current mindset.

Dealing with Shadows

Dark shadows can make it very difficult to see where certain puzzle pieces fit. As evolutionary development moves from stage to stage there are both healthy and unhealthy expressions that occur at each level. The healthy expressions are the strengths that become the foundation and springboards to higher levels, and the characteristics of prior stages that can be called upon effectively when necessary. On the other hand, the term 'shadows' refers to the unhealthy expressions that are dysfunctional and limiting. Shadows prevent true progress from being made because, when working on any type of maturity and growth initiative, these shadows will not allow themselves to be ignored. They will continue to raise their ugly heads at every turn and place roadblocks across the road to progress. Identifying these types of beliefs and behaviors as shadows allows efforts to be initiated that directly and openly address the dysfunctions so that subsequent growth and maturity can be enabled. Without stepping through the shadows and coming out the other side, the entire program is put at risk.

Shadows are the impediments to further growth that can exist on any developmental line, in any quadrant for any entity. Their disruptive tendencies can be seen at work through things like finger-pointing, antagonistic behavior, isolationist behavior, and rigid compliance. Below are some typical shadow behaviors for the first four stages of maturity:*

Stage	Shadows
Surviving	Blaming others, bullying, name calling and other demeaning behavior, physical posturing, intimidation, self-aggrandizement
Connected	Silos, lifelong employment, feelings of betrayal when a team member leaves, persecution for not explicitly following standard process, communication routing through hierarchy (up one side, across, then down the other)
Confident	Greed, materialism, consumerism and over-consumption, social inequality, reckless exploitation of resources, unethical behavior for profit, following 'fads' of higher stages
Purposeful	Acceptance and tolerance of bad behavior, 'like me, like us' shared ideals that limit diversity and inclusion, overzealous dismantling of hierarchy and structure

Much of these shadows have been developed and nurtured over long periods of time, so as part of the IMT assessment it is useful to go beyond the current state and investigate some of the history that led up to this point. It is in that history where you'll find something that has been disowned, denied or left behind. This is where many Modernization and Transformation programs fall short because during the process of implementing

---

* *Recall that moving to the '2nd tier' stages of Transparent and Intuitive have integrated all prior stages and therefore are not impacted by shadows as such*

specific changes in the areas of People, Process and Technology, consideration wasn't given to the history and current state of the organization's people, processes and technologies. This is *guaranteed* to lead to failure. By acknowledging that these problems exist and addressing the denied and disowned characteristics, shadows can be converted into collective acceptance and subsequently transcended. Therefore, the IMT assessment will bring these shadows out into the light and add specific efforts to the program that address them head on.

Work in Zones

At this point the program will have prepared the following:

- The IMT Vision Hypothesis (the custom image)
- The Transformation Office (the IMT team)
- The LPM Framework (the empty workspace)
- The Current State IMT model
- The Future State IMT model
- Identified Strengths
- Identified Shadows

Using these inputs, the next step is to identify the various activities that will move portions of the company closer to the future state. This activity will populate the LPM backlog to be prioritized which will in turn generate the roadmap for the program, but in the spirit of transparency, there first needs to be an open and honest discussion of the current state relative to the future state. Recalling the idea of an effort needing to be 'just challenging enough', the current state of the organization across all quadrants needs to be viewed with eyes wide open. Attempting to jump too quickly to some future state is rarely successful, so an approach of incremental progress is one that can be progressively built upon. Proposed program efforts should be identified as these incremental goals. The TO team can bring this current state 'reality check' to the executive team, who can then decide what efforts to mobilize first. The balancing act is in knowing when to push the envelope or not. Going through an exercise of prioritizing and sequencing the various proposed efforts will typically result in efforts 'bubbling' to the top of the list that address the IMT lines or charts that are furthest away from the future state and those that are inhibiting vision realization progress the most. The development lines with the least maturity (or identified shadows) will likely be where the most visible problems and opportunities lie. There will also be efforts to apply identified strengths in order to provide adequate support and guidance to increase the chances for success.

Similar to what was done for the IMT Vision hypothesis, the potential efforts on the LPM backlog can be framed as hypotheses as well. The goal of each effort is to make incremental improvement on a specific developmental line in the appropriate quadrant for a given entity – improvements that directly align to the customer, company and market needs encapsulated in the Vision hypothesis. Therefore, capturing the intent of the effort will help to determine if and when that intended outcome has been achieved. For example, *'If we establish and maintain automated regression coverage of >90% as part of our CI/CD pipeline, then we will reduce the number of defects introduced into the production system and reduce unexpected customer impacts',* or *'If we move our software development approach from temporary project teams to long-lived product teams, we will accelerate delivery of our product roadmaps'.* It is through the development of these types of outcome-oriented hypotheses that the specifics as to how they are achieved can be flexible, based on what is working and what is not.

For each of the identified maturity efforts, execution will differ depending on whether it is addressing interior or exterior aspects, or individual or collective pieces; yet almost every single effort will require some type of behavioral change. Many companies have minimized the amount of effort it takes to truly change behaviors, thinking that by sending their teams through training the transformation results will happen naturally. The teams that are trained may feel they truly grasp the new concepts in a classroom setting, but when they are sent back out 'into the wild' where demands and pressure to deliver come into play, they fall back to what they have done in the past. The end result is stagnation, not maturity. Even if new terminology is being used and people are outwardly 'going through the motions', the underlying behaviors have not really changed. Expecting people to become someone significantly different from who they are today, but not providing them the time and support mechanisms necessary to help them get there, is delusional at best, and more often negligent enough to guarantee failure of the initiative.

Leading an organization through Modernization and Transformation requires a more deliberate approach.

Each effort within an IMT program can be viewed as an intervention. The organization has a current set of habits and beliefs about themselves and the environment that requires reprogramming. Changing habits requires time and dedication, as it is known that it takes *at least* 21 straight days of doing something new before it becomes a habit, but *on average* it actually takes more than 2 months (66 days to be exact)[35]. Those timeframes also assume that the team and environmental structure is already in place and that any related training is complete. By not creating the space for employees to practice something new consistently over a good period of time, while neglecting to provide a safety net for them to stumble around a little bit until it becomes second nature, the risk is great because progress toward the intent of the program simply cannot be made. The chances for success go up significantly by being intentional and investing the time and effort it takes to help people through the change and also by alleviating as much stress as possible, as high stress levels cause 'relapses' and restart the clock. This is also where adding team members, or coaches who have the relevant skills and have 'been there and done that' can help provide support and guidance on a daily basis to the other team members. Support mechanisms can be established for ongoing development as well, such as spinning up Communities of Practice where practitioners across multiple teams and areas can share their experiences and advice. Immersing the team in an environment that supports them and creates the conditions for success will speed the progress of the overall initiative. Growth is enabled through learning, and learning new behaviors takes time, so doing everything possible to accelerate that learning is key to achieving the vision. Knowing that there is still an urgency behind the program, it is in everyone's best interests to minimize the amount of time it takes to establish new habits, understanding, and behaviors. When working within the program's LPM structure, assume that *nothing* will take less than 30 days, and will most likely take much longer. Modernization and Transformation programs are multi-year journeys that need to be managed with a long-term view in mind, but that still operate with effectiveness and efficiency in every short-term effort.

Running an IMT program demands that we keep in mind that this is an evolutionary initiative that requires a balanced approach across all quadrants and all lines. Tackling those areas that are least developed, 'shadowed', or require increased 'common understanding' is what enables progress to be made across all lines. Raising all developmental lines establishes a strong foundation for further maturity and growth that leads to realizing the ultimate vision. With the developmental lines guiding the categories of work to be done, efforts can be initiated that address any combination of values, needs, skills, technologies, rewards and recognition. These areas of focus become the 'zones' where multiple efforts are initiated and executed until adequate progress has been made. This means that periodically we need to step back a see how the overall puzzle is coming together.

Periodically Reviewing Progress

Running an IMT program is a collaborative effort between the Transformation Office and the executive team along with their respective staff. Therefore, there is a need for continuous communication and updates amongst the groups. Leveraging the LPM framework, the TO can keep the executive team informed of progress, with decisions being made around what initiatives to start, stop, or continue, based on available budget and bandwidth. Each effort moved from the backlog to 'in progress' will most likely align to a particular executive's area of responsibility, so they can take ownership of driving the work and providing color around what the TO team reports as progress.

Periodic reviews also support the evolutionary intent of the program and recognize the uncertainty of an unfolding journey. As learning will continue to happen and circumstances will change along the way, at each LPM checkpoint (typically held on a monthly cadence) there is a re-assessment of the vision and roadmap to ensure that they are still valid and that the various 'next up' efforts remain prioritized appropriately. One of the main objectives of re-assessing the vision and roadmap is to mitigate the risks that come from our natural cognitive biases. Due to the fact that LPM decisions are inherently infrequent and uncommon, they are very susceptible to anchoring, overconfidence, and confirmation biases. An anchoring bias '*is the tendency to fix on the initial information as the starting point for making a decision, and the failure to adjust for subsequent information as it's collected*'[36]. An overconfidence bias is the overestimation of being 'right' and assuming the first answer given, or the first plan laid out is the correct one. Confirmation bias leads us to gather information that confirms our initial conclusions and keeps us from fully examining the situation. These natural human tendencies lead to poor decision making as new information comes to light that should influence and change what was in the original plan. Consciously questioning if the original vision and roadmap still hold true, and assuming that they will indeed change over the course of the program, leads to better decision making and better program outcomes. This also leads to better flexibility in what should be the 'next up' efforts for the initiative.

Knowing that there will always be more work to do than afforded by available budget and bandwidth, another main theme of the LPM monthly reviews is to get the 'in flight' efforts to 'done' as quickly as possible. The mantra that keeps the program laser focused on completing the most valuable work that can be done at any given moment with the given resources is to 'Stop Starting and Start Finishing'. To help determine when an effort is 'done' the TO team can work with Data & Analytics teams to identify supporting metrics and create any reports or dashboards necessary to support the LPM decision making process. Any data that can be tied to the measurement of progress on specific developmental lines and quadrant maturity will be highly useful in determining if the associated hypotheses have been proven true or false. This creates and environment where LPM decision making can be both unbiased and data driven and keeps the flow of work moving at an optimal and sustainable pace. The picture of the future that the program sets out to build becomes increasingly clear as incremental progress is made and each piece of the puzzle is put into place, but what we then realize is that the image that is emerging is not the exact same one we started with. Something more organic is happening here. This is not a typical puzzle where we know exactly what the picture will look like when we are 'done'. In fact, 'done' may not exist at all.

The Next Generation Puzzle

There is a pattern that is frequently used when migrating to microservices from a legacy monolithic architecture that incrementally replaces existing functionalities with new applications and services in a phased approach. Piece by piece, component parts are put in place and the new application system eventually overtakes and replaces the entire legacy system. This is known as the 'Strangler Pattern' [37] or 'Strangler Fig Application'[38]. This is, in effect, the exact same approach that is happening when using the Integral Modernization and Transformation (IMT) technique. Just like a monolithic architecture, an organization is a complex legacy system that the IMT approach breaks down into its component parts, identifies the features and functions that need to be retained, replaces them one by one, then builds for the future on top of that. Given the fact that both the technology and the organization itself are the equivalent of complex adaptive systems, we know that the external environment around them is constantly changing and influencing the direction of their evolution concurrently with the internal IMT program. The puzzle we are solving for is of a picture that will be materially different than the one we defined as the 'future state' at the beginning of the Modernization or Transformation effort. There is no static image of what is to be built or achieved. The vision of what is becoming is more like a photo mosaic that shifts from one image to another over time.

A photo mosaic is a large image made from many small, tile-like colored pieces. It is different from a normal mosaic image in that the 'stones' or 'tiles' are also photos of other images themselves. This creates multiple dimensions in the image that is very similar to the holon concept used to describe the various levels of an organization. In a photo mosaic, the main image is the 'big picture', and the many individual images are the component parts that can be replaced individually without eliminating the illusion of the larger image.

By applying the strangler pattern, each photo could be replaced over time and a completely different large image may emerge that is entirely unlike the original. The evolutionary incremental changes are virtually invisible in the short term, but they support the creation of the new image over the long term, which may have *yet another* image that emerges beyond that. For companies that have begun a Modernization or Transformation program it is often viewed as something that, when finished, will finally provide them the new capabilities they need to survive. However, if they neglect their evolution again it will simply lead to the need for another painful and costly program in the future. What many organizations are beginning to realize is that their Modernization or Transformation initiative will never be 'done'. They need to stop viewing the effort as temporarily significant and shift to an approach of continuous and evolutionary modernization and improvement.

One of the main objectives of a Modernization or Transformation effort needs to be that another such program is never needed again. This can be accomplished by morphing the Transformation Office function into an Organizational Evolution Office. Using the IMT model in an ongoing basis, a growth cycle can be established using the same experimental attitude of the Lean Startup build-measure-learn cycle that uses an assess-identify-improve rotation. In the spirit of 'Adapt or Die' the organization that is constantly transforming is the one that will survive. Allow the big picture image to repeatedly morph into something new by providing the support structure to do just that.

Evolution is always in progress and the world is ever-changing. Time marches on and resistance to change is ultimately futile. Those organizations that do not mature and evolve will fade into history while those that embrace the temporary nature of what is will be best positioned for future success. By eliminating the need to do any Modernization or Transformation initiatives in the future you are staking your claim to the endless abundance that awaits. This is part of a shared evolutionary path that connects all of us as new entities come to life and contribute to the collective progression. Each company must go through the stages of maturity if they wish to remain a part of that journey. Otherwise, other companies will emerge to take their place at those higher stages. Each person, each team, and each company are connected to each other by this shared trek through time, every piece being a whole unto itself yet a part of another, with all of them coming together as one through an infinite number of links and interactions with each other. And we know these pieces fit.

Case Studies & Examples

This section provides several real-world examples of organizations that attempted various Modernization and Transformation initiatives but did not realize the expected value or were outright failures. For each case study, the following information will be discussed:

- Program Intent – what the company expected to accomplish
- Assessment Results – comparison of current state and future state using IMT modeling
- Strengths & Shadows
- Outcomes & Lessons Learned

These examples cover several decades of observations at multiple companies in differing industries. The IMT model is being applied in retrospect to highlight what could have been addressed as part of each program had it been available at the time. What ended up being 'lessons learned' after each of these unsatisfactory experiences could have been transformed into 'success stories' had a more complete and balanced approach been taken. Although the intent is to show how the IMT model can be used in practice, each case study is also a stark warning as to how easily a Modernization or Transformation can slip into the 'failure' column.

Healthcare IT Transformation

This company was experiencing problems with system stability and downtime. To address these issues, the program's intent was to establish new IT procedures, specifically creating initial project management and software development life cycle processes as well as new functions of quality assurance and software configuration management.

Assessment Highlights

As this was not an organization-wide initiative, the relevant starting point entity from an IMT model perspective was the IT processes that were a subset of the company's Employment quadrant. The best way to describe the IT processes at the beginning of the program was that they simply didn't exist. The IT organization was operating in a completely ad-hoc fashion with software developers working independently. They would manually drop new ColdFusion files into the production system by copying them from their local development environment file system. Whenever this created issues for users, either functionally or because it caused the system to go down, falling back to a previous system state was only possible if a single developer knew exactly which file caused the issue and could replace it with a prior copy. With the volume of daily file changes and the haphazard nature of how and when new files were copied to production, fall backs were rare and issues were typically handled in a 'fall forward' manner. The development teams embraced their 'cowboy coder' nature because they could operate autonomously and with minimal interaction with business representatives or the users themselves. Individuals who made heroic efforts to develop new functionality or address system issues, were rewarded accordingly via the annual bonus process. This process was handled through an excel spreadsheet manually created for each individual by each person's manager and filled out subjectively, often with language that benefited those that were adept at following orders and doing exactly what they were told by that manager doing the review. Using this combined information to generate a current state developmental lines bar chart produces the following:

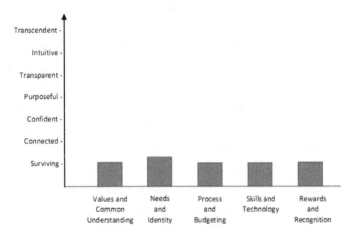

Extrapolating this out to an IMT quadrant diagram that represents the current state of the IT Processes:

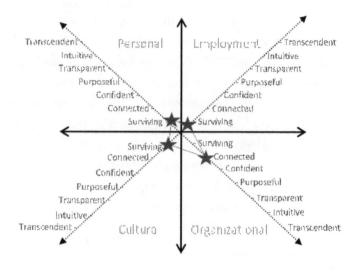

This diagram reflects that the organization overall was operating much like a governmental entity even though it was a privately held company. Any organization-wide policies or procedures that applied to or influenced the IT processes reflected a very bureaucratic hierarchy that had explicit roles and responsibilities defined across the broader scope which were very slow to change. Hence the Connected assessment in the Organizational quadrant. From the beliefs of the individuals and the teams themselves, formal IT processes were virtually irrelevant to how they operated on a daily basis. The lack of any formal documentation supported an assessment of Surviving across the other three quadrants.

Knowing this current way of operating was causing them problems, the IT department initiated the Transformation program to make changes that were to be wholly contained within the IT group, with no participation or interaction from other departments. The program was to establish clear roles and responsibilities, with appropriate separation of duties, that would be strictly adhered to, thereby reducing the risk of ongoing system outages. The future state of the IT processes was expected to be more in line with the broader organization:

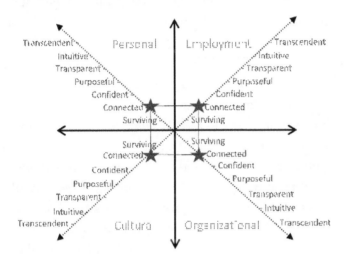

Strengths & Shadows

The IT department had a few employees with Project Management training, as well a single person with formal Quality Assurance and testing expertise. These people were augmented with new staff members to define, document, and publish the new Project Management and Software Methodology processes and procedures. New people were also hired to establish the beginnings of formal Quality Assurance (QA) and Software Configuration Management (SCM) teams that would be needed to support the new processes as defined. All of these people were being tasked out based on their skills and interests relative to the broader IT organization.

During the Transformation initiative it became increasingly clear that there was no support for the program throughout the IT leadership or extended management teams. Repeatedly scheduled meetings to discuss vision and alignment were not attended and subsequent detailed discussions and training were delegated to front line workers. It became clear that the impetus for the Transformation program was only superficially about addressing system stability and downtime. In fact, the underlying driver of the decision to build teams tasked with defining and supporting new processes was actually the poor perception of the IT department by the broader organization. In actuality, the motivation was all about the image of the leadership team and their desire to keep their jobs and stay in power. If IT could *show* they were taking corrective action, then their image would be preserved, but sadly there was no desire amongst the majority of the IT staff to actually change. The behaviors that were seen throughout the program kept the IT department 'stuck' at the Surviving level. The group continued to operate at this stage even through a major crisis where the patient care systems were down for almost 2 months because the new QA and SCM functions were bypassed, a fallback could not be accomplished, and multiple attempts to fall forward were unsuccessful. Those that tried to leverage the new processes and structures to address the crisis were perceived as being unsupportive and disloyal to the established powers that be, any many received reduced bonuses as part of their next annual reviews even though there were not specific line items in the spreadsheets that directly supported the lower ratings given. Most of the strengths that were hired in for the program left the company soon thereafter.

Outcomes & Lessons Learned

This IT organization was operating at the Surviving stage, an in a very unhealthy expression of that stage. The issues of being ad-hoc, individualistic, and fragile in nature could not be overcome without first addressing the shadows of the IT leadership and management team. These were shadows that they were not able to see in themselves and would have been completely denied and disowned had they been brought to light by anyone working on the program at the time. The fact that this Transformation was centered on IT processes alone and not viewed from a holistic and transparent standpoint across the broader organization, meant it was doomed to failure before it ever began. Had the effort been driven at the organizational level, with the participation and direction of the peers of the CIO and a broader assessment of more various and diverse IMT entities, outcomes could have been materially different.

Telecomm Software Modernization

This telecommunications software startup was looking to modernize their products' technology after heavily customizing the first-generation product with a large initial customer. This Modernization effort was specifically focused on changing from the client-server technology of the initial product to a web application architecture. The company itself had emerged from a technology consulting practice that identified a new market need that was not yet being addressed. As time was of the essence, the newly formed entity had utilized the existing skills and knowledge of those individuals and teams that made the move to the new organization in order to remain with the then President and CEO. The goal now was to learn new skills and rewrite the core application.

Assessment Highlights

Being wholly focused on the application technology, the starting point IMT diagram below represents the current state of the product and its client-server architecture. The individuals and team members that built this version were using the skills they had available at the time to create the product, but now felt that it was clunky, outdated, and hard to modify and maintain. The technical architecture itself was rudimentary in nature and leveraged what were well proven technologies and design patterns at the time. Organizationally, the technology was influenced by the opportunistic nature of the overall business endeavor the company represented. The current state of the application architecture is captured in the diagram below:

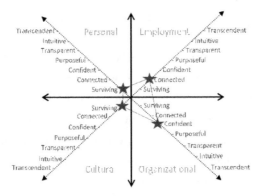

The intended future state of this software product was intended to be a more mature architecture that directly supported the organizational objectives while also allowing the delivery teams to establish new skills and expertise. The future state IMT diagram for the application architecture would then be the following:

The delivery teams that were building this product were divided between onshore and offshore groups. The onshore team wrote the system specifications and reviewed the delivered system, while the offshore team completed the detailed designs, coding, and testing. The onshore team believed that they needed to work quickly to seize the current market opportunity while the offshore team believed that they needed to do exactly what they were told (via documentation) by the onshore team. Meanwhile the company itself was operating with first round venture capital funding and had a single, albeit large, customer. They would need to attract more customers quickly if they were to stay in business. Moving up to the Organizational IMT diagram from the application architecture then, the current state would look like this:

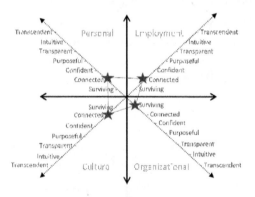

The Personal and Cultural quadrants shown above are average approximations of the combined teams, including the onshore and offshore delivery components. Drilling down into each of those provides a better understanding of the dynamics that were in play. For the onshore team, they believed not only that they were going to meet a current market need, but that they would be personally enriched by the experience as the initial employees of a startup with a strong potential upside. They also had the skills, tools, funding, and newly redesigned office space to support those beliefs, and even though they were still in startup mode, the pay was good. Visualizing this with an IMT developmental lines chart for the onshore team provides this view:

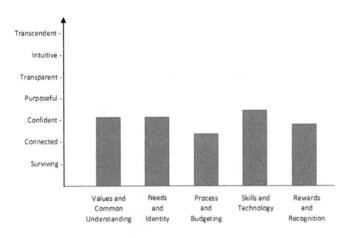

In contrast to the onshore team, the offshore team was operating at a very different level. They believed that they had to do exactly what they were told by the onshore team and follow, to the letter, the specifications literally, explicitly, and no more. This attitude came about because they had joined the new company as a show of loyalty to the CEO who was originally from their hometown where cultural influences dictated that they were now bound and subservient to him. As part of their 'do what you are told' mentality as well as a strict compliance to the documented SDLC process, each time a requirements specification was delivered there was an extended period of time of back-and-forth clarifications of the documentation that was captured and managed via spreadsheet. From a skill set perspective they had used what was already known and readily available to build the client-server version of the product and were now being self-taught with what was publicly available to build the web application version. Their pay and reward structures were mostly built on accepting whatever the CEO chose to route to their office and teams. Therefore, the offshore team's bar chart looked more like this:

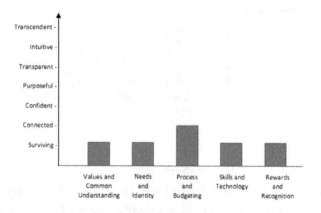

By comparing the two teams it can be seen why an average approximation of Connected was plotted for the Personal and Cultural quadrants of the Organization IMT diagram. The onshore team was operating closer to Confident, while the offshore team was at Surviving.

It is also worth noting another 'team' dynamic that was occurring, which was the influence of the first customer on the evolution of the product as well as the company itself. Having landed a significant contract with a sizeable customer, the organization treated that customer with near-absolute deference to their demands for customizations. The customer needs took priority over the company's needs, and much of the available manpower was directed at custom development and enhancements instead of prioritizing continued development of the core product. This limited the time and people available to build the new skills needed to move to the web application architecture, and also made the company very much bound to the licensing fees coming from an increasing number of customer users. An IMT diagram representing this customer would reflect those beliefs:

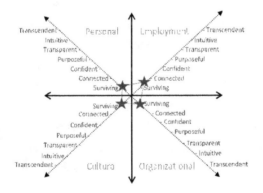

Strengths & Shadows

The strengths that this company had were in their capability to identify opportunities and gravitate toward them, both in the market need that was the company's genesis as well as being able to land a sizeable and distinguished first customer. However, the confluence of these two events highlighted the multiple shadows that were lurking behind the scenes when it came time to upgrade the application architecture.

The incapability of the offshore team to find their voice and become an equal member of the broader organizational team resulted in them being pulled to whatever the immediate demands dictated. The onshore team's drive for starting the company, quickly building the first version of the product, and appeasing the first client were rooted in a 'get rich quick' mentality that calculated the company would soon be sold or go public, resulting in a big pay day for everyone involved. The company's submission to the demands of the customer diverted resources from the maturation of the application architecture. The stark difference between the Confident nature of the onshore team and the Surviving nature of the offshore team resulted in a strong 'us versus them' mentality that was divisive and negative. With all of these shadows being allowed to run rampant, the outcomes of the Modernization initiative were ultimately predictable.

Outcomes & Lessons Learned

The Modernization of the company's application architecture never came to fruition. Although some progress was made toward the goal, the other issues that went unaddressed prevented the objective from being achieved and the organization itself filed for bankruptcy and was dissolved shortly thereafter. Had a holistic approach been taken across the entire organization, the impediments of the multiple shadows might have been able to be addressed so that the architecture, as well as the teams and the company itself, could have continued to grow and mature.

Global Travel Agent App Modernization

This global travel distribution organization was looking to build a more modern agency booking tool using new technologies and with a graphic user experience.

Assessment Highlights

This Modernization effort was initiated from within the Technology development area as a global expansion of a small regional solution that had been built a few years prior. Joining with the Product organization, the effort received approval from the top executives and a large development effort ensued. The existing booking tool in use by most customers at the time consisted of terminal access to mainframe systems that had been in use for several decades. Leveraging mostly cryptic command line 'green screen' functionality with associated scripting, global travel agents had become very practiced at interacting directly with the host systems. The Product and Technology groups believed that this solution was woefully out of date and if they were to increase their market share, a graphical user interface was necessary. Increasing market share was the primary concern as the company had been operating as a 'cash cow' for most of its existence. Therefore, the current state of the booking tool solution could be captured as:

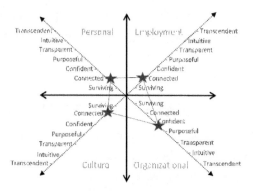

By modernizing the technology stack for the booking tool solution, the group expected to see lower development costs, advantages from hiring a workforce with current skill sets, easier product maintenance, and an uptick in usage and profitability. The future state of the booking tool product was intended to bring it more in line with the maturity of the overall organization:

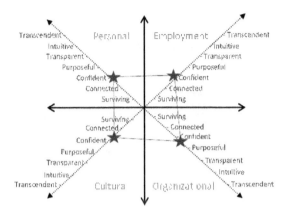

This organization had a well-established PMO and, working within a detailed AFE (Authorization For Expenditure) process dictated by Finance, generated detailed business cases and estimates for the program. When funding was approved, the assigned Project Manager began tracking progress against Waterfall milestones (requirements, design, coding, testing, etc.). As the effort progressed, a Red/Yellow/Green standard report was generated every month and reviewed by the Product and Technology executives, and also had visibility to the CEO. The project remained 'Green' for well over a year as scheduled milestones and waterfall approval 'gates' continued to be met and passed. All of this supported the assessment that the company overall was truly operating deep within the Confident stage:

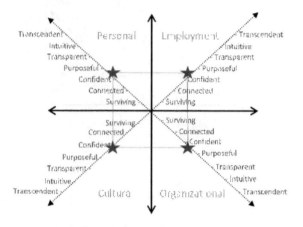

About 18 months into the project, when it was believed that enough functionality had been developed to accommodate the global user community as well as the extensive worldwide content (air, car, hotel, etc.), the Product team began the User Acceptance Testing (UAT) phase. It was at this point that there was a realization that even though the project milestones had all been hit so far, the functionality and the content had so many significant issues and gaps that the new product could not be rolled out in its current state. At this time, the project was supposed to complete the 2-week UAT, deploy the release package to the distribution site for customer downloads, and begin a 60-day warranty phase. Suddenly the project went from Green to Red and panic and finger-pointing ensued.

Strengths & Shadows

This organization had some very significant strengths that were added to the project. The Technology teams that had been pushing the envelope in using modern technology were leading the team, and other strong development and testing professionals were fully dedicated as well. The Product organization had a wealth of knowledgeable individuals that understood the details of every type of agency (subscribers) and travel content provider (suppliers). They had come together to make a next generation product that would be the envy of the industry.

However, their shadows were many and had become a deeply rooted part of their existence while the profits continued to roll in. Thinking they collectively knew all there was to know about the industry, the Product team believed they had supplied the exact requirements necessary for the Technology team to build the product. The Technology team believed they had mastered the new technology and could competently write a globally viable solution. In both cases their expertise had slipped into the shadow of arrogance. When issues began to arise, neither group could see that they contributed to the problem. The Product team blamed the Technology team for being 'slow and expensive' while the Technology team said the Product team failed to give them the right requirements. The PMO group also contributed to this in that they continued to track milestones per the schedule and did not pay attention to the grumblings that began to happen leading up to the first UAT. The combined Leadership teams were also laser focused on 'getting back to green' and trying to minimize the project timeline and budget overruns. The project was 're-baselined' several times while managing the effort relative to what was originally approved.

Outcomes & Lessons Learned

Approximately one year after the original UAT failure, the new agent booking tool product was launched, making it available for download by agencies around the world. Almost no one did. Throughout this entire initiative, across the hundreds of people involved from Product, Technology, and Leadership, nobody had done a detailed assessment of the customers. As commissions continued to be squeezed over the prior years, most travel agencies were working on shoestring budgets, with very little technology savvy, resources, or support, and they felt their value and expertise was in knowing the 'secret language' of the green screen cryptic commands. It was the 'one true way' to get at the best travel content and everyone at these agencies had been trained to do just that. For those that did have interest in the new product, they couldn't use it because their office systems hardware was running on old operating system versions that didn't support the new technology. They hadn't been investing any money into those types of things because they were simply trying to survive. Had an IMT diagram been compiled representing the Customers, it may have looked something like this:

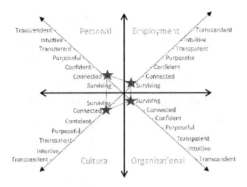

After investing millions of dollars, the product had minimal distribution and usage. The interesting thing beyond this particular Modernization effort was that it was just one in a trend of repeated efforts to do something other than the 'old green screen', yet the customers continued to use the older technology to simply stay in business, while the 'cash cow' company continued to sink funding into effort after effort with absolutely no positive effect on their market share. The company could very well have been better off financially to not have done anything at all.

Financial Services Agile Transformation

This company was transforming a group of approximately 2500 people to Agile ways of working with the implementation of the Scaled Agile Framework (SAFe).

Assessment Highlights

The new President of the organization declared that the company would be changing to Agile methods for delivery of all of their customer facing software solutions. The mandate included 'the business' as well as the IT development and testing teams. Since this was a completely process-oriented Transformation, the goal was to replace the previous Waterfall practices with Scaled Agile and using Scrum at the team level. The combined teams had been highly compliant with the previous methodology and brought that same mindset to learning and implementing the new processes. The organization overall had a very high level of risk aversion, which also influenced the environment of strict compliance to all policies and procedures. Looking at the current state SDLC processes had this type of diagrammatic representation:

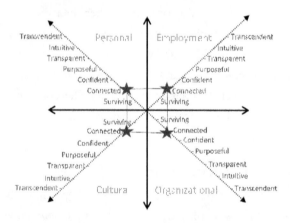

Knowing that 'true' agility is found at the Intuitive level, the future state of the development processes would have been targeting a significant leap in maturity in the Employment quadrant while retaining the core attitude of compliance to the new processes. This can be seen in the clearly skewed diagram below:

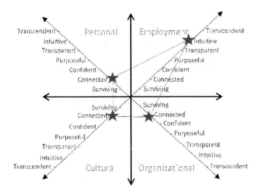

Moving up to the Organization level, the company was operating in a very structured and bureaucratic fashion. In order to prove compliance across the board, explicit documentation existed for how to do every operational function and clear roles and responsibilities were defined for every job role using RACI charts. Employees and teams believed in the rank-and-file structure of the organization and followed orders in military fashion. Therefore, the current state Organization chart reflected this full alignment with the Connected stage:

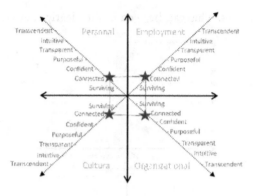

Drilling down into the IT teams that were being changed through this Transformation, they were working with multiple 'best-fit' technologies to support multiple customer channels, all built with a 'mobile first' approach. The management team was extensively using resource allocation spreadsheet to track the time and effort of each staff member to ensure that all of the requirements being supplied by the business were being addressed. While the individuals and teams still believed in 'following orders', the technology and project management portions of the environment were much more mature. The conflicting maturity levels of the developmental lines, and the resulting average approximation in the corresponding IMT diagram for the IT department looked more like this:

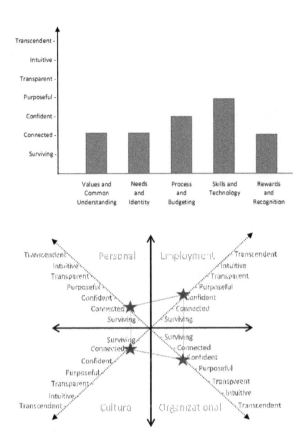

Drilling even further down into the individual level within the IT department, one of the top IT leaders had a clear set of developmental lines that significantly influenced how his teams behaved. This person was intentionally domineering and considered others to be a threat to their authority, actually taking an intimidating posture and aggressively questioning consultants as to why they were here and what problems they thought existed. Even though this person understood the diplomatic demands when interacting with the broader organization, they were very different when they were 'on their own turf' ruling their domain with an iron fist that team members knew not to cross. This person's developmental lines were mostly in the Surviving stage:

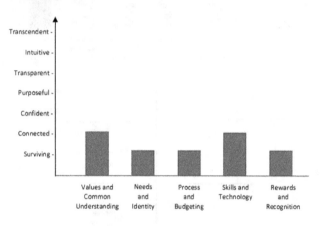

Although not as blatant as this particular individual behavior was, the executive team for the organization was also working at the Surviving level. Each executive identified themselves with how much budget and headcount they controlled, building business cases each year to claim as much of the available funding as possible and grow their teams. By the latter part of the year, those that were not overspent on their budgets would wield their power over others who came seeking assistance, and the back-office 'horse trading' would begin. This was treated as normal operations across the entire organization by the business teams reporting to these executives, and they would keep these negotiations private and confidential from the IT teams.

For these business teams, they kept a clear separation from the delivery teams organizationally, culturally, and physically. The business teams were housed in a completely separate building from their IT counterparts and there was not a convergence of reporting lines between the business and IT until reaching the President. IT was considered a 'cost center' that was there to deliver what the business teams commanded. Even during the Agile implementation, setting aside time for innovation 'hack-a-thons' was viewed as wasting valuable time needed for delivering what the business had on their backlogs. This significant chasm between the business and IT fully supported the Connected assessment in the broader organization.

Strengths & Shadows

This organization had significant technical talent. They produced products that were viewed as industry leading and had a couple of innovations that disrupted the competition and forced them to duplicate what this company had done in order to keep up. During the Agile Transformation initiative there were also several champions and enthusiasts that did what they could to help shift the behavior of the teams in the desired direction. However, for all of the strengths that existed they were no match for the inertia of the broader organization.

The environment that surrounded the technology teams was deeply rooted in the Connected stage, while the executive teams were mostly focused on acquiring and controlling more resources than their peers. When building the Agile Release Trains (ARTs per the Scaled Agile Framework standard model) those trains were not built as cross-functional teams that supported separate value streams. They were reflections of the organizational structure that existed leading into the Transformation, retaining the 'ownership' of the various IT teams by their business colleagues and their associated funding. The shadows that existed for the executives and business were dark enough to be completely blinding to the investment being made into Agile and the absolute lack of value they were realizing from the Transformation. The executives and business teams were quick to blame, bully, and intimidate others (especially IT) while self-aggrandizing themselves. Their penchant for maintaining their silos as 'fiefdoms' continued during the move to Scaled Agile, keeping key skills sets and knowledge separate from each other and slowing down delivery. As they were all operating at these levels on a day-to-day basis, they were trapped deep within their own maturity bubble and simply didn't know what they didn't know. Not being able to see the inhibitors as being within themselves, none of what was happening in the broader organizational environment was understood as being the factors limiting the intended progress in delivery maturity.

For the IT teams, the move to Scaled Agile gave them another method by which to show their conformity. Hundreds, if not thousands, of employees obtained multiple Scaled Agile certifications. The acronyms and badges for each certification were proudly appended to their email signatures. From an outward perspective the entire organization had embraced Agile and successfully completed the move to new ways of working.

Outcomes & Lessons Learned

This Agile Transformation was believed to be a success, and publicly claimed to be just that. Yet no measurable or material benefits were ever provided to support those claims. Given the limiting factors and shadows across the broader organization, this Agile Transformation had effectively been reduced to 'Agile Theater' where everyone had adopted a new vocabulary, performed all the scripted ceremonies, and presented an image of 'doing Agile'. In a way, this was exactly what was asked of them because the President who initiated the Agile Transformation provided no additional reasoning behind why they were pursing this path. The move to Agile was mandated, and the Connected nature of the organization resulted in immediate acceptance and compliance.

The evidence that this was actually a failing Transformation could be seen in their delivery metrics and dashboards. Each quarter the teams would go through massive Program Increment Planning sessions with hundreds of attendees coming together. The ceremonies were so large that they required booking offsite locations with all meals being catered for the teams. The spectacle was impressive. At these sessions, the teams would 'commit' to a plan for the next three months, stating exactly which features they would be delivering back to the business. Coming out of those meetings, delivering on the plan commitments became the dominant theme for the remainder of the quarter. The metrics that were used to report progress back to the business and the executives detailed exactly how many of the committed features had been delivered. Rarely was there a change in the 'PI Plan' where Agility was exercised based on new information or changing circumstances. The plan-driven nature of the organization had turned their so-called Agile organization into the agile anti-pattern known as the 'Feature Factory'. As long as the teams delivered the committed number of features, then they would effectively avoid the spotlight of criticism and blame. The Agile ceremonies had become the act to be performed for the audience, and the real work of scrambling to course correct to the original plan happened 'off the books' every day in the halls of the IT delivery center. None of the underlying behaviors and beliefs had actually changed and most of the people could not recognize this nor would they be able to admit it if they could see it.

The fact that failure was not an option, both in IT delivery and in the Agile Transformation itself, is a common problem in many companies. This could very well mean that the 75% failure rate of Modernization and Transformation efforts may actually be an underestimation.

Top 3 Bank Security Modernization

This company was compelled to rapidly change their security protocols across all customer channels due to a partner's data breach of customer PII (Personally Identifiable Information).

Assessment Highlights

The impetus for this Digital Modernization effort was the sudden exposure of millions of customer accounts to widespread fraud. The data that was stolen from a partner credit bureau included key pieces of information that this company used to verify and validate the ownership of customer accounts before providing access to funds and services. With an immediate threat to their customers bank accounts, as well as to their systems in general, this company needed to rapidly implement new tools and technologies to prevent the expected fraudulent activity. A large program was quickly initiated with extensive funding across multiple workstreams intended to address the various access points that were now vulnerable.

As the immediate need was to upgrade and reinforce technology-based access points, there were no related efforts to intentionally change anything in the 'People' or 'Process' domains. This program leveraged the company's standard approach to executing technology projects and expected those projects to be delivered by existing IT staff. The business stakeholders, in this case those concerned with fraud prevention, were tasked with identifying the various projects to be initiated and charged against the available program budget. At the outset of the program, initiatives were defined, business cases developed, and individual projects assigned to business-side Program and Project Managers. These managers were tasked with shepherding the projects through the internal processes, identifying risks to delivery, and providing status reports to the business stakeholders.

The 'Initiation' phase of the project management methodology included a monthly 'intake' process where the business could formally submit new projects to IT. As part of this phase, each project's estimated cost and expected delivery date was defined by the business stakeholders. For each project, the delivery target date was given as a fiscal quarter, e.g., Q1 2020. Once this information was deemed 'ready for intake', the Program and Project Managers would send the proposed scope, cost, and timeline information to IT for analysis. Over the course of the next month (prior to the next 'intake' date), IT would develop architectural designs, create milestone project plans, and staff the new projects accordingly through updating a comprehensive IT staffing model that supported the newly approved projects in addition to any existing 'in-flight' projects.

Due to the elaborate milestone (waterfall) project delivery methodology being used, combined with the amount of time dedicated to the initiation and intake processes, the minimum duration for any given project was 3 quarters (9 months), with most projects expected to take well over a year to deliver. Within the IT delivery teams, project plans were being broken down into 2-week sections termed 'sprints', although the complete Scrum model had not been fully implemented. Official Scrum teams did not exist because the staffing model assigned the same individuals to multiple concurrent projects, IT progress was not being reviewed at the end of each sprint, nor was the project plan adjusted based on new information. While the IT teams were beginning to adopt Agile vernacular, the projects were still executed with phase-gate milestones of design, coding, testing, etc. From a business perspective, there was not any transparency nor visibility into the specific delivery methods being used in IT. The status of each project was provided with a Red/Yellow/Green report using 'on time' and 'under budget' metrics. This report was created by IT Project Managers providing status to business-side Program and Project Managers who then prepared the readouts for business leadership and stakeholders. What was happening on the ground was being abstracted from the business stakeholders by several layers of reporting and managerial structures.

With the demand for strict process compliance as well as an 'Ivory Tower' approach to Enterprise Architecture, the Employment quadrant for this organization was deeply rooted in Connected stage. However, the business leaders and stakeholders displayed a certain level of aggressiveness as they coerced the IT teams to work within their original estimates of cost, time, and scope. This reflected lagging maturation in the Personal and Cultural quadrants, as the personal power dynamic acting in unison with a demand for strict compliance to processes and commitments revealed a level somewhere between the Surviving and Connected stages. The organization itself had been one of the largest and most profitable organizations for more than 150 years and was heavily oriented around doing everything possible to achieve quarterly financial targets, clearly placing it in the Confident stage of maturity. Therefore, the current state organizational chart was this:

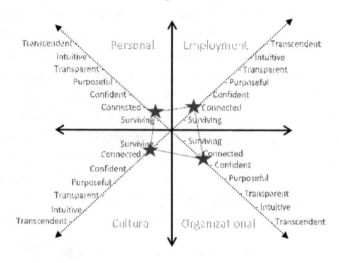

The goal of the Digital Security Modernization effort was to move the technology portion of the Employment quadrant to a higher level, leaving all other processes or environmental components as is. Therefore, the organizational diagram for the future state might reflect a slight movement of the Employment quadrant toward the Confident stage, but the average aggregation of the entire environment would make it nearly imperceptible.

The projects initiated in the technology space were to bring the Enterprise Architecture into the realm of biometrics, predictive telecommunication fraud detection capabilities, and enhanced authentication measures across all digital channels. Prior to this point the EA had been relatively monolithic in nature, and now needed to be componentized in order to leverage the new security and authentication information that would be flowing into, and between the systems. The original state of the EA in an IMT diagram representation was this:

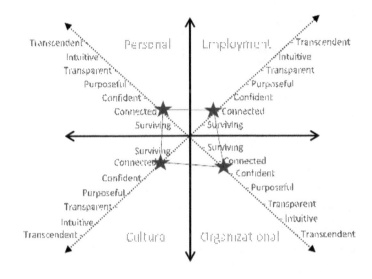

The objective of the program was to move to this:

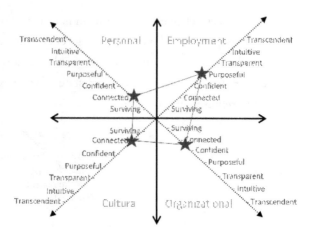

Strengths & Shadows

This company had many highly skilled fraud prevention people working for the business and they were very good at staying current on new security methods being used in the banking industry. On the IT side, there were many individuals that were working hard to bring new technologies into the Enterprise Architecture that could be leveraged across the entire organization. Unfortunately, the business strategy and the technology strategies were developed and pursued independently. This resulted in project estimates for scope, cost, and timelines to be defined with minimal IT involvement. For projects that were approved by the business, IT sought ways to fit the project requests into their pre-existing Enterprise Architectural vision. Both sides believed their thinking to be the 'one right way'. The amount of conflict and tension this created between the business and IT, even prior to this particular program, had created a toxic environment where battle lines were repeatedly drawn between the two sides. In one particularly notorious example, a particular project was running into problems early on and the threat of it taking longer than planned spurred some heated discussions. The main business stakeholder in charge of the overall program, on a conference call with a large number of attendees, angrily demanded of the IT leaders that their people start working nights and weekends in order to get the project back to 'Green'. There were 10 months left in the project timeline when this happened.

The toxic environment that already existed within the organization, which was further highlighted by the stress of an immediate threat to the company, resulted in a recurring 'Death March' theme where projects were roughly scoped, but estimates and timelines became commitments that could not be missed. This, of course, proved to be a fallacy as many of the slow-to-develop solutions simply could not be delivered 'on time' as the realities of what was needed continued to come to light. There were many instances where timelines were repeatedly delayed, scope was changed substantially, and money was spent on projects that were either ineffective or scrapped altogether. All the while, nobody was communicating openly as to the challenges that existed, as each project was 're-baselined' to show as 'Green'. In one instance, the business stakeholder meeting congratulated themselves for 'getting back to Green' by changing the plan, but not addressing the issues that continued to plague the effort.

Outcomes & Lessons Learned

Even though the program was utilizing process terminology and technology from other maturity levels, the beliefs and behaviors were still stuck between the Surviving and Connected stages. The discrepancies in maturity across the quadrants directly inhibited the realization of any true business value early on when the fraud threat was at its highest. Some of the technology improvements did come to fruition over a two-year period, despite the daily contentious environment, but even then, much of what was originally intended was never fully delivered. By not realizing the limitations in the current state of the Personal and Cultural quadrants, along with the non-technology components of the Employment quadrant, the organization spent hundreds of millions of dollars over an extended period with relatively little to show for it. Luckily, the stolen customer data never appeared on the Black Market or Dark Web as feared, and the company has been able to slowly continue their modernization without significant impact to their customer base.

Unfortunately, the organizational problems still exist as very little has been accomplished in the People and Process domains since that time. Had this company taken a more holistic approach that addressed the existing shadows and maturity levels, they might have been able to accelerate their delivery of valuable technology improvements and also prepare themselves to handle similar situations more gracefully in the future. Without a balanced approach to Modernization and Transformation, an existential threat still exists from within that fraudsters could easily take advantage of if they knew how much lead-time they would have between exploiting a vulnerability and the company effectively closing it down.

Patient Care Systems Modernization

This company was looking to replace fragile legacy patient care systems with a new technology stack while incrementally moving from an 'on-prem' data center to the cloud.

Assessment Highlights

This organization had been running the same patient care systems in their clinics for multiple decades. Over the years the systems had been hardened for the particular type of patient care they provided and were working well, but in order to expand to new methods of care, and the associated revenue streams, the platform architecture needed to be updated. In its current state the Enterprise Architecture was not capable of supporting the business strategy. Knowing that the future of the organization hinged on diversifying their offerings, the company set out on a multi-year Digital Modernization and Transformation effort that would become the basis for entering into new lines of business and enabling significant growth. The first step was to use a new technology stack to replace the existing systems, which was no small task.

The existing platform had grown from an originally ad-hoc environment and survived through the evolution of the organization and the acquisition by a new parent company. Over that time, an extensive amount of business knowledge had been codified within the systems themselves and they had in turn become highly trusted by the medical professionals that utilized them. In order to replace those systems, an exhaustive effort would be required to discover and replicate everything that was buried deep in the source code. Lives literally depended on it.

The leadership team at the time knew that the system replacement effort was going to be a significant investment that was estimated to take approximately 5 years to complete. The initiation of this program was also coming on the heels of some negative reviews from patients regarding their healthcare experience. Perhaps this was fortuitous since the planning for the program was highly influenced by the need to provide solutions that increased staff and patient satisfaction by transforming the 'customer' experience. The strategy for the program went beyond the technology modernization and targeted complete organizational transformation, intentionally creating an environment where this shift could actually occur. Planning efforts covered technology changes, corporate organizational changes, new IT delivery methods and team structures, and the creation of a pilot program that would provide ongoing feedback from healthcare professionals as to what was working and which parts were not yet ready for release. A new partnership between the business and IT was created that would jointly work with field practitioners during system design efforts and incremental system deployments to ensure that all parties knew exactly what was needed to make the system viable and trusted.

As this company had been in business for nearly 50 years, the transformational objectives of the program needed to address some things that had been in place for a very long time. What the leadership team decided to lead with was to build on the strong culture that already existed throughout the organization. Every employee believed their work to be valuable to their patient population, and internally they were working as a 'village' where they cared for each other with the same intensity that they cared for their patients. It was now time for their technology to mature in a way that would better support the company's mission and values. From a Personal and Cultural perspective, the organization was already working at the Purposeful stage. While the 'internal' aspects had been maturing, the 'external' aspects of the Employment quadrant, particularly processes and technologies, had lagged behind somewhere near the Connected stage. As the organization grew in size, reaching into the Fortune 200, the Confident stage had been fully attained which also reflected the midpoint between the maturity levels in the other quadrants. The organizational IMT diagram below depicts this starting state:

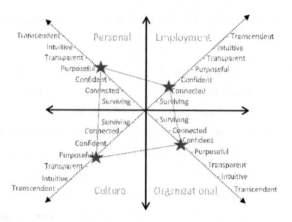

Having the combined objective to fully transform the organization, the goal was to bring the Employment and Organizational quadrants up to the Purposeful level of maturity, thereby creating a balance across all quadrants that would become the baseline for their longer-term growth strategy. This can be seen in the future-state organizational diagram below:

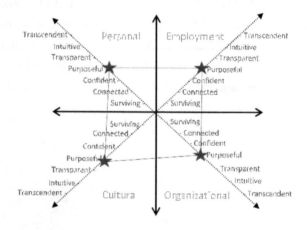

In order to accomplish this effectively, the IT group set out to adopt agile ways of working, implement DevOps development practices, and move from on-premise data center hardware to a prominent cloud provider, all while building a new system on a new technology stack. In each one of these areas the objectives were to shift from a Connected level of maturity to Purposeful. The new partnership between business and IT was leveraged to create a plan of incremental progress where changes in each area would be assessed on a quarterly basis and new changes initiated based on the success to date and new feedback received from the teams themselves. These feedback loops included frontline healthcare workers, IT development and support teams, business and product representatives, and the leadership team. After each round of feedback, an action plan would be created that included a monthly readout of progress against the new maturity objectives.

Strengths & Shadows

This organization had a distinct advantage in that the individual and collective 'internal' aspects had already spent significant time maturing into the Purposeful stage. The fact that nearly every single employee fully embraced the company mission and values allowed them to dedicate themselves to ensuring that this program would be a success. Over the course of the multi-year program the team members had little doubt, even during the most challenging times, that the Modernization and Transformation efforts would realize their objectives. Many extra hours were put in at various times, but this did not result in any burnout or feelings that this program would turn into a 'Death March'. The teams believed in their purpose and knew that the overall plan was to establish new ways of working that would ensure that a sustainable pace would be the norm going forward.

The main challenges that were faced were in the parts of the organization where certain roles were clearly being set on a path to become obsolete. For many years, the IT infrastructure was built and maintained in-house, with physical servers being procured, configured, operationalized, maintained, and retired with explicit policies and procedures. With this program being the trailblazer that would move a significant amount of their development, testing, and production systems to the cloud, the speed with which environments could be spun up and torn down showed that the old way of doing things would no longer support the needs of the business. Change was happening and there was clear resistance to the transformation that presented itself as risk aversion to the 'unknowns' of operating in the cloud and protecting patient data.

Outcomes & Lessons Learned

Although the program lasted for more than the anticipated 5 years, the Digital Modernization and Transformation was profoundly successful. By proceeding with an attitude of 'we don't know what we don't know', the iterative and incremental approach to making changes across every aspect of the organization allowed for course corrections to be made and for late adopters to be brought onboard through the use of empirical evidence. For example, the resistance seen from the IT infrastructure teams was overcome by using small pilot projects to prove that the governance and controls necessary to address the legal, risk, and compliance needs of the organization could be achieved in the cloud environment. Internal systems were targeted to be repurposed, and a training program was initiated to bring many of those infrastructure employees new skill sets that were needed to support the new enterprise architecture.

What may have been the key that unlocked success for this program was the time they gave themselves to learn and adapt. Each set of incremental changes, whether it was regarding organization structure, new processes, or new technologies, was given anywhere from 3 to 6 months to take root before building more on top of that base. The fact that executive leadership were able to release their focus on the originally planned timelines in the name of making sure the program was doing what was 'right' for everyone involved helped set the conditions for success. Taking a very 'human-centered' approach to the program that considered the needs of employees, healthcare practitioners, and the patients themselves allowed them to be mindful of what was truly needed across all areas of transformation. With the success of the program as it approached General Release for thousands of locations, the company began looking to the next phase where they could evolve the newly built platform to extend their business in new ways and establish new products and revenue sources. The balanced approach across the four quadrants truly transformed the business, and it will continue to transform, piece by piece, for the foreseeable future. This company knew how to make the pieces fit.

Endnotes & Further Reading

[1] It Is Not the Strongest of the Species that Survives But the Most Adaptable - https://quoteinvestigator.com/2014/05/04/adapt/#:~:text=Claren ce%20Darrow%20once%20said%2C%20%E2%80%9CIt,one%20m ost%20adaptable%20to%20change.%E2%80%9D
[2] 2019 CEO Survey: The Year of Challenged Growth - https://www.gartner.com/en/documents/3906929/2019-ceo-survey-the-year-of-challenged-growth
[3] Digital Transformation Success Is NOT Rooted in Technology - https://www.everestgrp.com/2019-09-digital-transformation-success-is-not-rooted-in-technology-blog-51242.html#:~:text=Here's%20a%20sobering%20fact%3A%20Everest,%2C%20even%20worse%2C%20abandoned%20projects.
[4] Why do most transformations fail? A conversation with Harry Robinson - https://www.mckinsey.com/business-functions/transformation/our-insights/why-do-most-transformations-fail-a-conversation-with-harry-robinson
[5] 74% Of Organizations Fail to Complete Legacy System Modernization Projects, New Report From Advanced Reveals - https://www.businesswire.com/news/home/20200528005186/en/7 4-Of-Organizations-Fail-to-Complete-Legacy-System-Modernization-Projects-New-Report-From-Advanced-Reveals
[6] Digital Transformation Is Not About Technology - https://hbr.org/2019/03/digital-transformation-is-not-about-technology
[7] Light ICO. The Cost of Digital Transformation. https://www.lightico.com/blog/the-cost-of-digital-transformation/
[8] 14th Annual State of Agile, 2020 - https://www.stateofagile.com
[9] 35,000 Decisions: The Great Choices of Strategic Leaders - https://go.roberts.edu/leadingedge/the-great-choices-of-strategic-leaders

[10] The Relationship Between Complexity and Behavioral Bias - https://repository.upenn.edu/cgi/viewcontent.cgi?article=1018&context=mbds

[11] Beginning with this section, the approach and method being proposed pulls heavily from Ken Wilber's Integral Theory, particularly the All Quadrants, All Lines (AQAL) philosophic model laid out in his books Sex, Ecology, Spirituality: The Spirit of Evolution, Shambala Publications, 1995 and Integral Spirituality; A Startling New Role for Religion in the Modern and Postmodern World, Integral Books, 2006.

[12] Frederic Laloux. Reinventing Organisations: A Guide to Creating Organisations Inspired by the Next Stage of Human Consciousness. Nelson Parker.February 9, 2014

[13] Integral Life. Ten Stages of Human Consciousness: Stage 7 – Relativist (Self-Questioning) https://integrallife.com/ten-stages-consciousness/

[14] Reinventing Organizations Wiki. Green Paradigm and Organizations. https://reinventingorganizationswiki.com/theory/green-paradigm-and-organizations/

[15] Daniel Pink. Drive: The Surprising Truth About What Motivates Us. Riverhead Books. December 29, 2009

[16] https://reinventingorganizationswiki.com/theory/green-paradigm-and-organizations/#fn4 "The first major study dates from 1992, when Harvard Business School professors John Kotter and James Heskett investigated this link in their book Corporate Culture and Performance. They established that companies with strong business cultures and empowered managers/employees outperformed other companies on revenue growth (by a factor of four), stock price increase (by a factor of eight) and increase in net income (by a factor of more than 700) during the 11 years considered in the research. A more recent study by Raj Sisodia, Jagh Sheth, and David B. Wolfe, in … Firms of Endearment: How World-Class Companies Profit from Passion and Purpose—came to similar conclusions in 2007. The "firms of endearment" studied by the authors obtained a cumulative return to shareholders of 1,025 percent over the 10 years leading up to the research, as compared to 122 percent for the S&P 500."

[17] Gallup CliftonStrengths
https://www.gallup.com/cliftonstrengths/en/252137/home.aspx
[18] Maja Roosen. How to Reward in Self-Managed Teams.
https://www.linkedin.com/pulse/how-rate-reward-self-managed-teams-maja-roosjen/
[19] Complex Adaptive System – Wikipedia.
https://en.wikipedia.org/wiki/Complex_adaptive_system
[20] A description of Jean Gebser's 'Integral' stage of consciousness from the presentation "Jean Gebser THE EVER-PRESENT ORIGIN Power Point Presentation for the Seminar on Psychology of Social Development organized by the University of Human Unity"; https://slideplayer.com/slide/8536045/
[21] Shuhari – Wikipedia. https://en.wikipedia.org/wiki/Shuhari
[22] Yuval Noah Harari. Sapiens: A Brief History of Humankind. Vintage; 1st edition 30 April 2015; Homo Deus: A Brief History of Tomorrow. Vintage; 1st edition 23 March 2017
[23] This discussion pulls heavily from Ken Wilber's works on developmental lines and the use of psychographs in his book Integral Spirituality; A Startling New Role for Religion in the Modern and Postmodern World, Integral Books, 2006.
[24] Capability Maturity Model – Wikipedia.
https://en.wikipedia.org/wiki/Capability_Maturity_Model
[25] Cynefin Framework – Wikipedia.
https://en.wikipedia.org/wiki/Cynefin_framework
[26] Colton Swabb. The Hermetic Revival: 7 Ancient Principles For Self-Mastery. https://medium.com/the-mission/the-hermetic-revival-7-ancient-principles-for-self-mastery-9399e523648d
[27] Emerald Tablet – Wikipedia.
https://en.wikipedia.org/wiki/Emerald_Tablet
[28] Agile Alliance. Niko-Niko Calendar.
https://www.agilealliance.org/glossary/nikoniko/
[29] Burke Litwin Model of Change.
http://changemanagementinsight.com/burke-litwin-model-of-change/
[30] Enterprise Architecture Assessment Framework (EAAF).
https://obamawhitehouse.archives.gov/omb/E-Gov/eaaf

[31] Atlassian Agile Coach. Lean Portfolio Management.
https://www.atlassian.com/agile/agile-at-scale/lean-portfolio-management
[32] Corporate Finance Institute. What is Beyond Budgeting?
https://corporatefinanceinstitute.com/resources/knowledge/finance/beyond-budgeting/
[33] Scaled Agile. Portfolio Kanban.
https://www.scaledagileframework.com/portfolio-kanban/
[34] Zapier. The 7 Best Online Whiteboards in 2021.
https://zapier.com/blog/best-online-whiteboard/
[35] James Clear. How Long Does it Actually Take to Form a New Habit? (Backed by Science). https://jamesclear.com/new-habit
[36] Lumen. Biases in Decision Making.
https://courses.lumenlearning.com/wm-organizationalbehavior/chapter/biases-in-decision-making/
[37] N Natesan. How to use strangler pattern for microservices modernization. https://www.castsoftware.com/blog/how-to-use-strangler-pattern-for-microservices-modernization
[38] Martin Fowler. StranglerFigApplication.
https://martinfowler.com/bliki/StranglerFigApplication.html
[39] Mona Lisa Photo Mosaic Image.
https://www.fiverr.com/sjrm75/create-a-photomosaic-of-any-image-you-want